GROWING LITTLE WOMEN

for
younger
girls

9.00

*T*his book is a gift of love from _____

to _____ on _____

I want to spend time with you over the next few weeks because _____

_____

_____

_____

_____

_____

_____

_____

_____

_____

Signature *Katia-Lee GI*

GROWING
LITTLE
WOMEN

for younger girls

*Capturing Teachable
Moments with
Your Daughter*

Donna J. Miller
Christine Yount

MOODY PRESS
CHICAGO

All Scripture quotations are taken from the *Holy Bible, New International Version*®. NIV®. Copyright © 1973, 1978, 1984 by International Bible Society. Used by permission of Zondervan Publishing House. All rights reserved.

Library of Congress Cataloging-in-Publication Data

Miller, Donna J.
  Growing little women for younger girls: capturing teachable moments with your daughter / Donna J. Miller and Chistine Yount.
      p. cm.
  Includes bibliographical references.
  ISBN 0-8024-2942-4
  1. Mothers and daughters. 2. Motherhood—Religious aspects—Christianity. I. Yount, Christine. II. Title.

HQ755.85 .M54 2000
306.874'3—dc21

5 7 9 10 8 6

Printed in the United States of America

Dear Jennifer and Tracy,

    I can vividly remember the day each of you were born.

    I recall two distinct feelings—first, being overwhelmed with the thought of responsibility as a mother, and, second, being thankful for the wonderful privilege to be part of your lives.

    You both have truly been gifts from God. What joy and delight you've brought into my life.

Love,

Mom

    To my mother, my mentor, and my friend. Your life continues to challenge me to seek Christ first and live to serve Him.

I love you,

Donna

    To my mother for teaching me that hard work is its own reward; that honesty is the best policy; and that no sacrifice is too great for children. I love you this much (arms held open wide)!

Christine

    And to my daughter Abby—precious princess who came into this world with a mixture of delicacy and strength. I delight in watching you become a little woman whose heart seeks after God.

Mom

CONTENTS

Acknowledgments   11
Dear Mothers   12
Dear Daughters   14
Being Your Daughter's Mentor   15
Why Do We Meet?   15
How to Use This Book   16

Section One
Developing the Best Me

Week 1: I'm Special!   23
Week 2: R-E-S-P-E-C-T   35
Week 3: Being Brave   43
Week 4: Saying "Thank You"   51

Section Two
Others and Me

Week 5: Making Friends   63
Week 6: Choosing Leaders   71
Week 7: Come to My House   81
Week 8: Saying "I'm Sorry"   91

Section Three
Knowing God

Week 9: Belonging to God   101
Week 10: Talking to God   109
Week 11: Listening to God   117
Week 12: Telling Others About Jesus   125

Section Four
Doing What's Right

Week 13: Telling the Truth   137
Week 14: Kindness Counts   145
Week 15: "Because I Said So!"   153
Week 16: A Gift from Mom's Heart   161
Certificate of Completion   172
Certificate of Commitment   173
Twenty-one Questions   175
More Fun Stuff   183

ACKNOWLEDGMENTS

*T*hank you to the following people who made this book possible . . .

- Jim Bell for his sensitive coordination and support in bringing this book to life.
- Brigit Bell for her perfect illustrations.
- Suzanne Dowd for knowing each of us well enough to realize that we would love working together.
- And our families for their untiring and loving support in any venture we undertake for the kingdom of God.

Dear Mothers,

In 1985, my husband and I started meeting with a small group in our church to study a course on lifestyle evangelism. It was especially challenging and exciting for me as I learned how to discuss my faith in a nonthreatening way with unbelievers. At the end of this course, we were all assigned to target three or four people to witness our Christian faith to. If we were able to lead them to Christ, we were to disciple them afterward.

During the next few weeks, I asked the Lord to lead me to the right people and to prepare their hearts to receive Him. Each time I prayed, my older daughter, Jennifer, came to mind. I kept praying.

After a few weeks, I finally got the hint. The toughest challenge of all—to disciple one of my own children. I immediately began collecting resources and ideas to use in my discipling time with Jennifer. A few years later I discipled my younger daughter, Tracy.

How I would love to sit down with each of you and tell you what the months of discipling my daughters have meant to me. Even though the active time of discipling is now over, I can still see the positive effects it had on each of us. It is clear to me that the time we spent together in those formative years strengthened our relationships in their teenage years. Our time together bonded us to each other and laid a foundation of open communication, helping us establish mutual trust and loyalty that grew into a warm, lasting friendship.

As a mother, it is very important that you first examine your own heart before you begin discipling your daughter. I encourage you to be absolutely certain that you have a relationship with Jesus Christ and know Him personally as your Savior and Lord. If you are not sure whether or not you know Him or you don't know what I mean, I am asking whether you have ever told God you know you're a sinner, you can't save yourself, and you accept Jesus Christ's death on the cross as the payment and forgiveness of your sins. (See John 3:16.)

Chapter 9 has a chance for you to ask your daughter if she has ever made this important decision. Even if you are quite sure of her standing with God, ask her to articulate the decision that she has made. If she has not done so, you may want to wait until later to go through this book with her or use that chapter in an earlier week.

As the mom, you will set the tone for your time together, so be relaxed and expect to have fun! There is no right or wrong way to go about it. The important thing is not whether you complete a chapter each week. The goal is for you and your daughter to get to know each other better and for you to share a part of yourself with your daughter. The time you spend together is an investment in developing her character and instilling meaningful values. The result is that the two of you will grow together as you learn more about the Lord and each other.

Your daughter will not be perfect because of your time together, but you will see the Lord teach her in many ways through your time together. Christine and I pray that you and your daughter will grow together in the Lord and in your friendship.

Your daughter will probably never be the same again . . . and neither will you.

Donna Miller

3 John 4
I have no greater joy than to hear that my children are walking in the truth.

Dear Daughters,

It was my privilege to have special time with my mom when I was a young girl. I am excited that you get to have this experience with your mother.

Many of the things I learned have stayed with me for many years. That's especially important this year because I will be completing high school and heading off to college.

The time with my mom taught me that God has a hope and a future for me—just as He does for you. Jeremiah 29:11 is my life verse: "'For I know the plans I have for you,' declares the LORD, 'plans to prosper you and not to harm you, plans to give you hope and a future.'"

My mom and I also had special outings that deepened our relationship. My prayer for you is that you will have a fun and meaningful time together, with many great memories. And believe it or not, you will even teach your mom some things!

Love in Christ,

Tracy Miller

BEING YOUR DAUGHTER'S MENTOR

All children love to play follow the leader. Whatever the leader does, the follower does in the exact same way.

That's what it means to be a mentor to your daughter. You lead and she follows. As your daughter follows you, what will she see? Will she understand why you do what you do? Will she know without question what you believe?

The apostle Paul was not afraid to say, "Follow my example, as I follow the example of Christ" (1 Corinthians 11:1). *Growing Little Women for Younger Girls* will enable you to say the same thing to your daughter.

WHY DO WE MEET?

- so my daughter and I will get to know each other better; to spend special time together one-on-one; and to discuss my values with her.
- so my daughter will gain more insight about her identity in Christ and begin to think about her future. I'll try to answer her questions about her Christian walk and why we believe as we do.
- so that each of us will learn more about the Lord and grow spiritually.
- to build her character for the future.
- so that our relationship will grow stronger and I can show her how much I love her.

HOW TO USE THIS BOOK

*F*irst of all, you need to begin praying for the time when you will be discipling your daughter. Then, little by little, introduce the idea to her. Don't just announce your plan. Ask her how she feels about getting together once a week for a special time just between the two of you. It is important that she looks forward to doing this with you.

Mom, you will set the tone for your time together. If you are excited and enthusiastic about the idea, she will likely feel the same way about it. So remember:

Be fun!

Be creative!

Be committed!

The lessons have material for approximately one to two hours. They are meant to be used for sixteen consecutive weeks. Don't feel that you have to answer every question in every lesson—stick with what is helpful for you and your daughter and the amount of time that works for her attention span. We have also provided a section called "Twenty-one Questions" for you and your daughter to go through and answer—encouraging your relationship even more. Chapters include additional activities (called "Action Ideas") that can be done at a separate time during the week or even saved for a later date. Some of these apply to the lessons of the week; some are just ideas of ways you and your daughter can spend time together. The end of the book also has a section called "More Fun Stuff" if you are looking for other excuses to do things together.

Plan to begin at a time when you will be able to follow through each week. Choose a time when pressures at home are reduced. For some that might be summertime; for others, after school begins in the fall. But pick a time when you're less likely to be running a family of kids to Little League or music lessons or somewhere else. Schedule this hour into your week and make it a priority, or it simply won't happen on a regular basis.

Each chapter begins with a Scripture reading to get you thinking about the topic, then a short story relating to the theme for that week. These stories are designed for you to read aloud to your daughter. It may have been a while since you've read a story to her, but reading to her will nurture her soul. Don't underestimate the impact this will make on your success.

Try to make time to read the story in advance of your meeting time so that you will be familiar with it. Then read it aloud with inflection and lots of drama. Your daughter will love this special attention. This will give you a chance to savor a quiet moment in her fleeting childhood.

Once you've read the story, read and discuss the questions that follow. These three or four questions will help to get both of you talking about the story and subject for the week. Then help your daughter look up and read the verses in the Bible as she fills in the blanks in "What Does the Bible Say?" Notice that we have used the *New International Version* of the Bible; it will be easier to know what goes in each blank if you use the same version.

All of this leads us to the heart of the book—discussing and applying these scriptural truths to your daughter's life today. This section of each chapter is where you will become closer to your daughter as each of you tells your thoughts. We've provided space for you to document your discussion. This section is called "Looking Deeper." Some questions are mainly for the mother, some for the daughter, and some for both of you. Each chapter closes with a memory verse for the week and a prayer.

In the process of working through this book, you'll come to better understand your daughter, while at the same time passing on to her timeless principles. Personalizing the book will give her a keepsake of your time together.

One way this book will be personalized is by your own stories, experience, wisdom, and knowledge of your daughter. Many of these sessions will probably be intimate hours for the two of you.

Chapter 16 may be the most important chapter in the book. It is your chapter to personalize—filled with a lot of blank spaces designed to give you a chance to tell your daughter a story of your own. That might be a story about how you met and fell in love with her father. You may choose to tell her how you came to know and accept Christ. You might want to tell her about something else meaningful in your life or hers. We've titled this chapter "A Gift from Mom's Heart," because this truly is the best gift you can give your daughter—a piece of your own heart and a chance to celebrate and mark the closing of your special time together.

Other places that need your personal touch include the presentation page (in the front) and the certificate of completion (in the back). The first is a personal note from you to your daughter; the second is a ceremony to celebrate all that you've accomplished in completing the book together.

We have attempted to craft this book for girls between the ages of seven and ten. But girls develop at varying speeds during these years. You know your daughter best and understand her emotional and spiritual development. For this reason, we ask you to read through each week before engaging in it with your daughter. Plan ahead. Resist the temptation to just sit down and begin the lessons. Read or at least scan the chapters to get an idea where you're headed in this adventure. The important thing is to think through the materials and be comfortable with them before you start.

If you feel she is not yet ready to deal with the concepts or subject matter in any particular chapter, skip past it to another. In fact, feel free to skip around or change the sequence of topics as you feel necessary to make your time with her special.

The important thing is that this time bonds you together with warm moments worth keeping and celebrating. Sharing this special one-on-one time early in her life may set the tone for the years to come. We hope this time you and your daughter have together will be the beginning of a wonderful, lifelong relationship. Once you're finished with this book, we hope that you'll enjoy spending time together in the *Growing Little Women* book for girls from ages nine to twelve.

You'll never regret the time you've carved out to be together, and neither will your daughter.

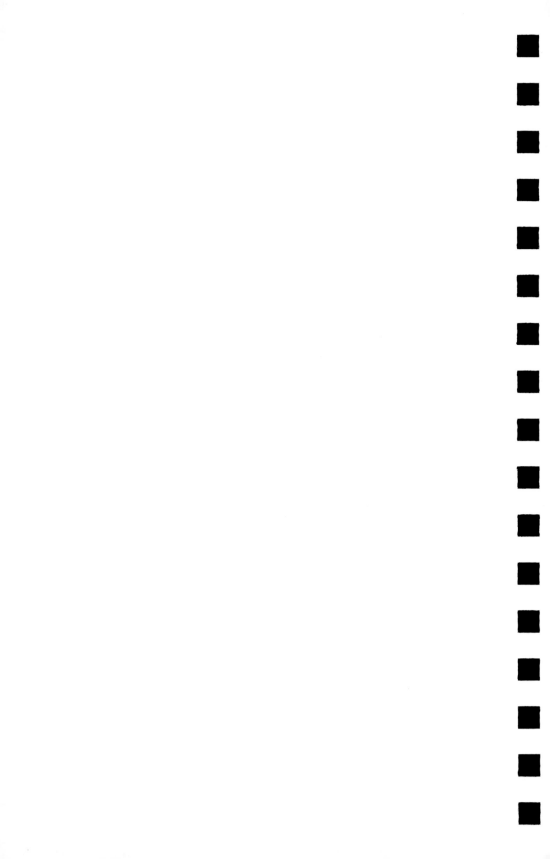

Section One

DEVELOPING
THE BEST ME

Week 1

I'M SPECIAL!

Scripture Reading for This Week

Psalm 139:13–17

For you created my inmost being; you knit me together in my mother's womb. I praise you because I am fearfully and wonderfully made; your works are wonderful, I know that full well. My frame was not hidden from you when I was made in the secret place. When I was woven together in the depths of the earth, your eyes saw my unformed body. All the days ordained for me were written in your book before one of them came to be. How precious to me are your thoughts, O God! How vast is the sum of them!

These verses tell us what God was doing with you when you were inside your mother. How do these verses show that you are special to God?

Daughter: _____

Mom: _____

How does that make you feel?

Daughter: _____

Mom: _____

*F*rom the very moment that I knew my first baby was beginning to grow inside me, my mind could think of nothing else. I couldn't stop smiling!

I knew that tiny speck of life was a gift from God. I wondered what the next eight or nine months would hold—for sure, nothing I'd ever experienced before. I felt excited but also a little scared. Everything was so new to me, but I knew that God promised to be with me and to take care of the little one growing inside me. And believe me, my baby was growing!

As each month passed, I got even more excited. I could see my tummy getting bigger and bigger. I could feel the little person inside me moving around. Sometimes I'd feel a little hard knot at the top or bottom or side of my belly. I wondered if I was feeling my baby's arm, leg, or head. Sometimes I would just sit, not only feeling my stomach move, but also watching it! My baby was really active even before birth. I wondered if my baby was a girl or a boy. I wondered what he or she looked like.

Lots of times I asked myself if I was ready to become a mother. I would have to take care of my baby all of the time—not just when I felt like it. I'd have to teach my baby to eat. I'd have to feed the baby every two or three hours, even at night. I'd have to keep the baby clean and dry and warm. I would have to figure out if the baby was sick—and what to do about it. I would have to show my baby every minute that I loved her. I'd have to show her and tell her that God loved her too. Even if I got sick, I would still have to take care of my baby. I wondered if I would be ready for all this work. I wondered if I would know what to do.

I read everything I could find about babies. I read a lot about how to be a good mother. I talked with my friends who already had babies. I discovered that I really liked to talk with my mother about babies. After all, she'd done a good job of taking care of me. She gave me special tips on babies and being a parent. But what I remember most was our times praying for my baby. We prayed that the baby would grow just right, that she would be healthy, that she would be born at just the right time and in just the right way, and that God would help me take care of her. My prayers helped me feel that God would help the baby and me to be ready for each other.

The last few months moved fast. I decorated the nursery all yellow because I wanted my baby to see bright, sunny color in her world. I hung yellow curtains at the window and put a yellow sheet in the crib. My favorite spot was the corner where I put a rocking chair. Sometimes I sat there and rocked, singing softly to myself and to the baby in my tummy. I imagined how happy I'd be someday soon when I could sit in that same chair and cuddle my baby in my arms. I was ready. The nursery was ready. Everything was ready. Now I simply had to wait until my baby was ready too.

Finally that special day came—the day my baby Jennifer was born. She was born early on a Saturday morning. She had been alive inside me for nine months, but now the baby I had been carrying inside was lying in my arms. It was so exciting! I touched her tiny face—it was more beautiful than any face I'd ever seen. I touched her rosy cheeks, which were so soft I was almost afraid I'd hurt her. I stroked her hair, which was dark and wispy all over her head. All I wanted to do was hold her close. As I held her, gently cupping her tiny hands and feet in my hands, I wondered what her hands would create and where her feet would run.

Holding my baby for the first time was one of the happiest moments of my life. During those first moments, I felt a special bond between us. I knew then that I would always love her. I asked God to help us continue the sweet relationship we had in those first hours in the years to come. I'm so thankful that God gave this beautiful little girl to me.

What the Story Says
1. God made you.
2. God knows you.
3. God loves you.

Discussion Questions

For Mom:

1. Tell your daughter her birth story—from the beginning. (If your daughter is adopted, tell her about the special day you brought her home.) Write a few highlights to answer the questions below.

2. What were your thoughts when you learned that a baby was growing inside you?

_____

_____

_____

3. How did you feel when you held your daughter for the first time?

_____

_____

_____

4. How did you choose your daughter's name?

_____

_____

_____

5. What special things did you do to prepare a place for your daughter in your home?

   _____

   _____

   _____

6. Tell your daughter what you especially liked about her when she was tiny.

   _____

   _____

   _____

7. Point out what you especially appreciate about your daughter as a person now. (Hint: Aim for character qualities rather than outward appearances.)

   _____

   _____

   _____

For Both:

Use page 28 for do-it-yourself art. Gather crayons, chalk, colored pencils—whatever you like to draw with. Show a favorite part of what happened when your daughter came into your family. For example, you may draw people who visited you or who held her, what she looked like, her favorite toys, how she was dressed, what kind of place the family prepared for her, or how your family celebrated her birth. Have fun!

> *The day of your birth was special.*
> *When you were born,*
> *your family celebrated.*

_____

(Your Name)

_____

(Your Birth Date)

What Does the Bible Say?

GOD MADE YOU AND GOD KNOWS YOU

For Mom:

Read Psalm 8:3–9.

³ When I consider your heavens, the work of your fingers, the moon and the stars, which you have set in place, ⁴ what is man that you are mindful of him, the son of man that you care for him? ⁵ You made him a little lower than the heavenly beings and crowned him with glory and honor. ⁶ You made him ruler over the works of your hands; you put everything under his feet: ⁷ all flocks and herds, and the beasts of the field, ⁸ the birds of the air, and the fish of the sea, all that swim the paths of the seas. ⁹ O LORD, our Lord, how majestic is your name in all the earth!

For Daughter:

1. Name some of the things that God made.

   _____

   _____

2. Look at verses 6 through 9. What does it mean to rule over the things listed in these verses?

   _____

   _____

For Both:

1. What are some ways that you can take care of what God has made?

   _____

   _____

2. What is the most wonderful of all God's creation?

   _____

   _____

3. Why do you think people are more important to God than anything else that He created?

   _____

   _____

Mom, open the Bible and help your daughter look up the following Scriptures and fill in the blanks.

Psalm 139:14
I praise you because I am _____ and _____ made; your _____ are wonderful, I _____ that full well.

Luke 12:7
Indeed, the very _____ of your _____ are all _____.

Jeremiah 31:3
I have _____ you with an _____ love.

For Mom:

What does God mean when He tells us that He loves us with an everlasting love?

_____

_____

_____

For Daughter:

1. Draw a head beside the verse that shows you that God knows you.

2. Draw a heart by the verse that shows that God loves you.

3. Draw hands beside the verse that reveals that God made you.

Looking Deeper

For Mom:

What is special about your daughter?

_____

_____

_____

For Daughter:

What is special about your mom?

_____

_____

_____

For Both:

What makes you special to God?

_____

_____

_____

Action Ideas

• Pull out family photo albums. Find photos of your daughter for each of these categories.

Who I was . . .
(find a photo)
Who I am . . .
(find a photo)
What I like to do . . .
(find a photo)
Who I'd like to be . . .
(write or draw your goals and dreams)

• Do a star-watch together. On a clear night, take pillows and blankets outdoors. Stretch out and get comfy. Look for special stars and constellations. Talk about how big the stars are, how far away, and how old. Remember that God made the stars—and you! And God thinks that you are even more important than anything else He has made.

Words to Memorize
For we are God's workmanship, created
in Christ Jesus to do good works.
Ephesians 2:10

Your Goal for This Week

_____

_____

_____

Closing Prayer

Lord, thank You that You
made me and know all about me.
I am very thankful
that You love me so much.

Week 2

R-E-S-P-E-C-T

Scripture Reading for This Week

Ephesians 6:1–3
Children, obey your parents in the Lord, for this is right. "Honor your father and mother"—which is the first commandment with a promise—"that it may go well with you and that you may enjoy long life on the earth."

These verses tell us about a promise. What is this promise?

Daughter: _____

Mom: _____

What do we have to do to receive this promise?

Daughter: _____

Mom: _____

$\mathcal{T}$he summer after Chris finished fourth grade was a busy one. She had almost three months filled with fun activities! During this summer Chris decided she really wanted to please God in every way.

Chris had always loved sports, but she did not know exactly which ones she liked best. So she played on three different teams that summer. She swam on the swim team, played basketball, and played softball.

Chris loved playing softball. She felt so important playing the games at the high school's softball field. They played under the lights as parents and friends in the bleachers cheered them on. This was Chris's second summer to play softball, so a lot of her friends from school were on the team.

Chris was excited to be a part of the Otters team again, but especially this summer because her friend Kara's dad would be the new coach. Mr. Baxter was so friendly. He was always smiling, and he was easy to talk to. He really seemed to enjoy the girls, and they could sense it. Mr. Baxter never yelled or got angry at them if they dropped the ball or struck out. He was always encouraging. He was just what Chris needed in a coach, since she was not very confident in softball.

As the season went on, Chris noticed how Kara spoke to her dad, Mr. Baxter. Kara rolled her eyes at him and talked back in a hateful tone of voice. And sometimes she even laughed at her dad right in front of the other coach and her teammates. Kara didn't seem to care what she said to her dad. She definitely did not understand the word *respect*.

During the softball season, Chris became less interested in her friendship with Kara. Chris said it made her sad to see Kara treat her father so terribly.

The Otters ended with a winning season—not one loss! A lot of the team's success was due to Mr. Baxter's coaching and encouraging words. Each girl on the team was given an individual trophy for being on the first-place team, but Chris was given much more. She saw that what she had been taught at home and at church about respect was very important. Seeing Kara's lack of respect, Chris decided that she wanted to show respect to her parents and other adults.

After the last game, Chris asked her mother if they could stop by the store and buy Mr. Baxter a card. Her mother gladly said yes. Chris carefully chose a card for Mr. Baxter. Shortly after they arrived home, Chris came out of her bedroom with the card.

Her mother read what she had written in the card. "Dear Mr. Baxter: I want to thank you for coaching the Otters team. You are a great coach. You're so nice to all of us on the team. I also think you are a special dad too. Thank you, Chris."

What the Story Says

Others respect you
when you respect others.

Discussion Questions

For Mom:

1. Tell your daughter what it means to respect others.

2. Tell your daughter about a time you noticed her attitude of respect.

3. When you were your daughter's age, how did you show respect to your parents or other adults in your life?

For Daughter:

1. List two reasons it's important for you to show respect to others.

1. _____

2. _____

2. Write the names of three people you want to show respect to. Ask God to help you show respect to these people.

1. _____

2. _____

3. _____

Mom, stage a puppet show with your daughter. You can use ready-made puppets, or you can make your own. You can make simple puppets from paper bags or even just by gluing buttons and a felt smile to an old pair of socks. With your puppets, act out these scenarios:

- After church, the pastor shakes your hand as your family leaves. How do you show respect?
- You're watching your favorite TV show, and your mother tells you to turn off the television and clean your room. How do you show respect?
- A neighbor tells you to clean the trash out of his yard even though you did not put it there. How do you show respect?

What Does the Bible Say?

Mom, open the Bible and help your daughter look up the following Scriptures and fill in the blanks.

1 Peter 2:17
Show proper _____ to _____: Love the brotherhood of _____, fear God, _____ the king.

1 Thessalonians 5:12
Now we ask you, brothers, to _____ those who work _____ among _____, who are _____ you in the Lord and who admonish you.

Who at your church fits this verse? How can you show respect to these people?

Romans 12:10
Be _____ to one another in _____ love. _____
one another above _____.

What does it mean to "honor one another"?

Matthew 19:19
"_____ your father and _____," and "_____ your
_____ as yourself."

Looking Deeper

For Mom:

Tell your daughter about a time when it was hard for you to
respect someone. Summarize it below.

_____

_____

_____

For Daughter:

Tell your mother about a time when it was hard for you to respect
someone. Write it below.

_____

_____

_____

For Mom:

Is it possible to respect someone in authority but not respect the
person's actions? Explain your answer below.

_____

_____

_____

For Daughter:

If you had been Chris, what would you have said to Kara?

_____

_____

_____

For Mom:

List the people in your life whom God has called you to respect.

_____

_____

_____

Tell your daughter three things that you respect about her. Write them below.

1. _____

2. _____

3. _____

Talk with your daughter about how these things can help others respect her.

_____

_____

_____

For Daughter:

Tell your mother three things that you respect about her. Write them below.

1. _____

2. _____

3. _____

Action Idea

Chris wrote a letter to someone she respected. Each of you, write a letter to someone in authority that you respect. You could write a letter to your husband or father, a school principal, boss, pastor, or someone else.

Words to Memorize

Children, obey your parents in everything,
for this pleases the Lord.
Colossians 3:20

Your Goal for This Week

_____

_____

_____

Closing Prayer

Dear Jesus, help me to show respect and honor to my parents and other adults in my life. I want to obey Your Word.

Week 3

BEING BRAVE

Scripture Reading for This Week

Psalm 91:1–2, 4, 9, 11

[1] He who dwells in the shelter of the Most High will rest in the shadow of the Almighty. [2] I will say of the LORD, "He is my refuge and my fortress, my God, in whom I trust." . . . [4] He will cover you with his feathers, and under his wings you will find refuge; his faithfulness will be your shield and rampart. . . . [9] If you make the Most High your dwelling—even the LORD, who is my refuge . . . [11] he will command his angels concerning you to guard you in all your ways.

Daughter: Who will keep you safe? _____ What are some ways He keeps you safe? _____
_____

Mom: Verse 4 says, "He will cover you with his feathers, and under his wings you will find refuge." Explain what this means to you.

$\mathcal{I}$t was May 28. There were only two days of school left before summer vacation. Caroline sat at her desk daydreaming about summer. She had enjoyed third grade and her teacher Mrs. Nelson, but now she was looking forward to everything she would be doing this summer. Well, she was looking forward to everything except church camp.

Caroline could hardly wait for the bell to ring so she could ride the bus home. She wanted to talk with her mother about church camp. It was only two weeks away, and this was Caroline's first year to be old enough to attend. She was excited and a little nervous at the same time. What would it be like to be away from her home and family for five days at church camp?

Caroline's leader at girls' club was excited that so many of the third-grade girls had signed up for camp. She had been talking with them since January about camp. The leader said she knew the girls would have fun and learn a lot too.

Caroline was afraid to let her leader know that she was worried about going to camp. She wanted to talk to her mother. She knew that she could always talk to her mother about anything. When Caroline got off the bus after school, she told her mom that she was afraid of being homesick at camp.

"Let's go get some ice cream," her mom said. Mrs. Bradford could see that her daughter was upset. As they sat enjoying their ice cream and special time alone, Mrs. Bradford told Caroline about all the exciting things that she would experience at church camp.

"At first you might be a little lonely for your family," Mrs. Bradford said. "Then you'll have so much fun sleeping with the other girls in your cabin, being in skits, and playing games. You'll make neat crafts each day, sing songs, and hear exciting Bible stories."

"Will I get to swim?" Caroline asked.

"Yes! Every afternoon!" her mother exclaimed. "And during one of the evenings, you'll have a campfire."

"I'm afraid I won't know anyone," Caroline admitted.

"Many of the camp counselors and other leaders are from our church," Mom assured Caroline. "And remember, Patty, LaShonda, and Monique are all going."

As they finished their ice cream, her mother said, "Caroline, I have something special for you." She reached into her purse and pulled a card out of her wallet. She told Caroline, "Whenever I need to be brave, I pull out this card and read it."

She handed the card to Caroline. "I want you to keep it with you this summer," Mrs. Bradford said. "And if you ever feel afraid, you can pull it out and read it too."

Caroline read the card aloud: "The LORD is my light and my salvation—whom shall I fear? The LORD is the stronghold of my life—of whom shall I be afraid?" (Psalm 27:1).

Caroline gave her mom a big hug. "Thanks, Mom! I feel better now," she said.

What the Story Says

Wherever I go, and whoever I am with,
the Lord will take care of me.

Discussion Questions

1. How did Caroline feel about church camp?

_____

_____

_____

2. Why do you think Caroline felt this way?

_____

_____

_____

3. What made Caroline feel better?

_____

_____

_____

For Mom:

We need to trust the Lord with our fears. The word "trust" means confidence and faith. Tell your daughter about a time you were afraid but you trusted the Lord. Write it below.

_____

_____

_____

What Does the Bible Say?

Mom, help your daughter look up the following Scriptures and fill in the blanks.

Psalm 34:4
I _____ the _____, and he _____ me; he _____ me from _____ my _____.

Isaiah 41:10
So do not _____, for I am _____ you; do not be _____, for I am _____ God. I will _____ you and _____ you; I will _____ you with my righteous right _____.

Who is always with us? _____

Psalm 118:6
The _____ is with me; I will not be _____.

Isaiah 41:13

I am the LORD, your God, who takes _____ of _____ right _____ and says to you, Do not _____; I will _____ you.

Psalm 121:7–8

The LORD will _____ you from _____ harm—he will _____ over your _____; the LORD will watch over your _____ and _____ both _____ and forevermore.

Read Psalm 121:7–8 together. Thank God that He always watches over you.

Looking Deeper

For Daughter:

Have you ever been afraid? What did you do when you were afraid?

_____

_____

_____

_____

What scares you?

_____

_____

_____

_____

How can remembering that God is with you help you be brave?

_____

_____

_____

_____

For Mom:

Tell your daughter about something that scared you when you were her age. How did God help you overcome your fear?

_____

_____

_____

For Both:

Pretend that Caroline is at camp and she writes you a letter about her fears. Together, write her a one-paragraph letter to encourage her to be brave.

_____

_____

_____

_____

_____

_____

_____

_____

_____

With your daughter, make a plan for how you'll help her when she is afraid. Write your plan.

_____

_____

_____

_____

Take turns praying for each other. Ask God to help you be brave by remembering that He is always with you.

Action Ideas

Buy a pair of white pillowcases. Use colored permanent markers to decorate the pillowcases with your names, favorite Bible verses, pictures, and anything else that will remind you to brave. Be sure to put a big piece of cardboard in each pillowcase first, so colors won't bleed through to the other side. You can use these pillowcases to take to camp for the first time, to a church retreat, or for an overnight sleepover.

Words to Memorize

For he will command his angels concerning you
to guard you in all your ways.
Psalm 91:11

Your Goal for This Week

_____

_____

Closing Prayer

Dear Jesus, thank You for taking care of me and watching over me. Help me to trust You when I am afraid.

Week 4

SAYING "THANK YOU"

Scripture Reading for This Week

Psalm 100:1–5
Shout for joy to the LORD, all the earth. Worship the LORD with gladness; come before him with joyful songs. Know that the LORD is God. It is he who made us, and we are his; we are his people, the sheep of his pasture. Enter his gates with thanksgiving and his courts with praise; give thanks to him and praise his name. For the LORD is good and his love endures forever; his faithfulness continues through all generations.

When King David wrote this psalm, how was he feeling about God?

Daughter: _____

Mom: _____

Psalm 30:12
That my heart may sing to you and not be silent. O LORD my God, I will give you thanks forever.

For Daughter:

What are three other words or phrases for "forever"?

_____

For Mom:

Why should we "not be silent" but give thanks to God?

_____

_____

I'll never forget the day that Jesus touched me. No one had touched me in years. No back rubs. No hugs. No one even held my hand.

I was shuffling down the road early in the morning. I had to find something to eat in the garbage areas.

Plop, plop. Shuffle. Shuffle.

"Uh-oh! Run and hide!" my friend yelled to me.

Voices and footsteps were coming our way. We looked from side to side, but couldn't find any place to hide. There were ten of us that day hunting for food. It was not easy to hide ten people.

But we had to hide. We were lepers. Some of us only had one or two of the white sores on our bodies. Yet some of us had lost our fingers and toes to this terrible disease that ruined our flesh. Healthy people didn't like to look at us, so we always hid when we heard other people coming.

For years we had lived together—far from anyone who didn't have this disease. I missed my family so much, but I could never go back to see them. If I touched them, they might catch my leprosy.

It was against the law for us to touch "clean" people. That's what they called people who didn't have leprosy. I was "unclean" —covered with rotten skin.

Now we could see a group of four or five travelers coming over the hill. They were walking toward us. We stumbled to the side of the road. My friend James squinted his eyes. "I think I know that man's name," he said, "the one in the middle."

"Who is He?" I asked.

"His name is Jesus. He's some kind of teacher. And He can heal us if He wants to," he explained.

As Jesus and His friends came nearer, we held out our hands to Him. We had all heard that Jesus had healing powers. Many people believed He came from God.

"Jesus, help us!" my friends cried out.

"Jesus," I whispered. I turned away when He looked my way. I didn't think I was good enough for Jesus to even look at me.

Jesus stopped. He did not reach out to touch us. Instead, He spoke with the kindest voice I had ever heard. "Go, show yourselves to the priests," Jesus said.

The priests! I thought. The priests were the ones who made us stay away from everyone. But then I remembered the Law said the priests could tell if someone was healed from leprosy.

Before Jesus could even turn to go, all ten of us started toward the temple. There was something in Jesus' voice that made us want to do whatever He said. Some of my friends limped; some hobbled. We tried to help each other along.

Soon, everyone was running fast. No one limped. No one hobbled. We looked down at our skin. All the white spots were gone. We were healed.

I was so happy, I was crying. I was healed. My friends ran even faster toward the temple, but I stopped right in my tracks. Jesus had healed me!

I turned and ran back to Him to say thank You. My life would never be the same because of what Jesus had done for me. I could go home now and live a normal life. My heart overflowed with thankfulness.

I was puffing and panting by the time I reached Jesus. I

could barely speak. I fell before Him, and I huffed the words, "Thank You, Jesus! Thank You!"

His eyes were full of love when He spoke. He held out His hands and pulled me up. I could see that He delighted in me.

He threw His arm around me and turned to the people who had crowded around Him. "Weren't there ten who were healed?" Jesus asked. "Is this man the only one who returned to give thanks to God?"

Jesus was surprised that I had returned because I wasn't even one of the people who believed in God before this happened. I knew that Jesus was pleased because I had stopped to say thank You.

The last thing Jesus said to me that day was "Your faith has made you well."

—*story adapted from Luke 17:11–19*

What the Story Says

Jesus is happy when we
remember to thank Him.

Discussion Questions

For Mom:

Tell your daughter a little more about leprosy. Be sure to explain that doctors have found a cure for leprosy, so it's not really a scary disease anymore.

For Daughter:

1. Suppose you and nine of your friends had a terrible

creepy, crawly skin disease all over your body. How would you feel?

_____

_____

2. What would be hard about living with that kind of disease?

_____

_____

3. How did Jesus help the leper in this story?

_____

_____

_____

For Both:

Why do you think this man was the only person who came back to thank Jesus? How do you think Jesus felt when this man said thank You?

_____

_____

What Does the Bible Say?

Mom, help your daughter look up the following Scriptures and fill in the blanks.

1 Thessalonians 5:18
Give _____ in all _____, for this is God's _____ for _____ in Christ Jesus.

Ephesians 5:20

_____ giving _____ to God the Father for _____,
in the _____ of our Lord Jesus Christ.

1 Chronicles 16:34

Give _____ to the _____, for he is _____; his
_____ endures _____.

God wants our praise and thankfulness. He does not make us thank Him, but He is pleased when we do.

Looking Deeper

For Both:

Why is it important for us to say thank You to God?

_____

Why is it important for us to say thank you to people?

_____

What can you thank God for today?

_____

For Daughter:

Draw three things on the following page that you can thank Jesus for.

For Both:

After your daughter draws the three pictures, create a border of words around the pictures. Take turns writing things that you're thankful for, and create a frame of words all the way around the pictures.

List three ways that you can help each other be more thankful.

1. _____
2. _____
3. _____

For Mom:

Tell your daughter why you're thankful for her. Write it down.

_____

_____

_____

For Daughter:

Tell your mom why you're thankful for her. Write it down.

_____

_____

_____

Action Ideas

- Write a note of thanks to a Sunday school teacher, neighbor, friend, or schoolteacher. Make cookies to deliver with the note.

- Make a "Blessings Bag." Decorate a small brown bag. On separate slips of paper, write things you're thankful for and put the papers in the bag. Take one out each day this week and thank the Lord.

Words to Memorize

Give thanks in all circumstances, for this
is God's will for you in Christ Jesus.
1 Thessalonians 5:18

Your Goal for This Week

_____

_____

_____

Closing Prayer

Lord, help me be thankful for You, my family, and all that You give me. Amen.

Section Two

OTHERS AND ME

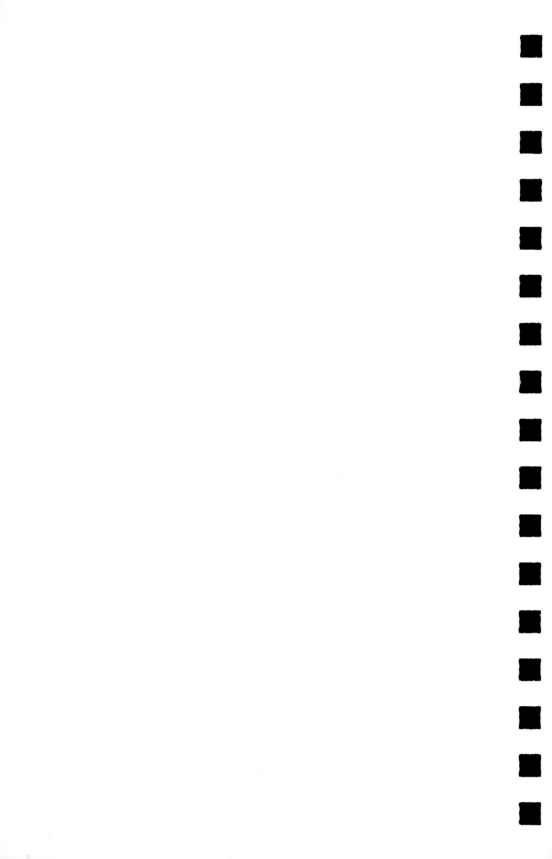

Week 5

MAKING
FRIENDS

Scripture Reading for This Week

Proverbs 12:26
A righteous man is cautious in friendship, but the way of the wicked leads them astray.

Mom: What does it mean to be cautious in friendship?

_____

_____

_____

How can you choose your friends carefully?

Mom: _____

Daughter: _____

*W*hen Grant entered the fourth grade and met Josh, he immediately knew that he wanted to be this boy's friend. He told his mother that he wanted to lead Josh to Christ, and he often talked to Josh about whether he believed in Jesus.

The boys lived in the same neighborhood, so they walked home together after school. Several days when Grant got home after school, he told his parents that kids had hit him or said mean things to him.

"What happened?" they asked Grant.

"Kids were making fun of Josh."

"Well, why did you get hit?" his parents asked Grant.

"I wasn't going to let them hurt Josh, so I stepped in to protect him."

Sometimes Grant was "protecting" Josh from middle-school kids who were much bigger.

Grant's parents wanted to support Grant in his efforts to be a good friend to Josh, but it seemed that Grant was having problems on the way home more and more often. Finally, they talked to the principal about it. What they learned was a big surprise.

"Josh is in trouble constantly here at school," the principal explained.

"Yes, Grant told us that kids are mean to him," his mother said.

"That may be true, but Josh brings most of his problems on himself."

Grant's parents learned that Josh usually said something to make other kids angry, and then he expected Grant to jump in and protect him. Josh sometimes used bad language, and he said things that were hurtful to others.

This conversation opened Grant's parents' eyes to Josh's character. They told Grant that he couldn't walk home with Josh any longer and that he needed to evaluate whether he should be friends with Josh or not.

Grant was sad when his parents told him that his friendship with Josh would need to change if Josh did not change. And Josh was sad when Grant explained his parents' concerns to him.

Yet Josh did not change. And Grant began to see that Josh was not the kind of boy that he wanted to be friends with. In fact, the more time Grant spent away from Josh, the more he saw what Josh had been doing to other people.

Grant learned a big lesson about choosing friends carefully. Grant is still usually friendly to Josh, but he doesn't consider Josh one of his best friends anymore. They rarely spend time together now.

What the Story Says

Be friendly to everyone,
but choose your friends wisely.

Discussion Questions

For Both:

1. Why do you think Grant's parents weren't sure whether Grant should be friends with Josh anymore?

_____

_____

_____

2. Tell your daughter about a friendship you had as a child that did not work out.

_____

_____

_____

For Daughter:

Tell your mother about a person that you thought would be a good friend but really wasn't.

_____

_____

_____

For Both:

1. What makes someone a good friend?

_____

_____

_____

2. What makes someone a bad friend?

_____

_____

_____

For Daughter:

Write a poem about your best friend.

What Does the Bible Say?

Mom, help your daughter look up the following Scriptures and fill in the blanks.

Psalm 119:63
I am a _____ to all who _____ you, to all who _____ your _____.

What does this promise to God mean?

Proverbs 17:17
A _____ loves at all _____, and a _____ is born for _____.

Ecclesiastes 4:10
If one _____ down, his _____ can _____ him up. But pity the _____ who _____ and has no _____ to help him ____!

Looking Deeper

For Both:

Look up and read 1 Corinthians 13. What does the chapter list as character traits of a person who loves others?

_____

_____

For Mom:

Which of these traits are hard for you?

_____

_____

For Daughter:

Which of these traits are hard for you?

_____

_____

Action Ideas

- Each of you make an award for your best friend. Use construction paper and markers, stickers, or rubber stamps. On your award, write the qualities of your friend that you appreciate the most.
- Take your best friends out for lunch and present the awards to them. Thank them for their friendship and pray together, thanking God for such good friends.

Words to Memorize

A righteous man is cautious in friendship,
but the way of the wicked leads them astray.
Proverbs 12:26

Your Goal for This Week

_____

_____

_____

Closing Prayer

Dear Jesus, help me to choose my friends wisely. Thank You for the special friends that You have given me.

Week 6

CHOOSING LEADERS

Scripture Reading for This Week

Proverbs 3:5–6
Trust in the LORD with all your heart and lean not on your own understanding; in all your ways acknowledge him, and he will make your paths straight.

Mom: What does "with all your heart" mean?

_____

Daughter: If we acknowledge the Lord, the Bible tells us God will make our paths _____.

Mom: Does "straight" mean that everything will go our way, always be perfect, and we won't have any problems? Explain.

_____

Tell your daughter what you think this means: "Lean not on your own understanding."

_____

_____

Draw a timeline of your life from birth to now. Point out the times that you clearly sensed that God had led you, such as decisions you've made regarding your career, marriage, or faith.

$\mathcal{T}$he bell rang and all the kids ran out of Mrs. Haley's fourth-grade class. Jessica couldn't wait to play with her friends at recess. But when she caught up with Kathryn and her other friends, they were huddled beside the swing set.

"What's going on?" she asked.

"Come here," Kathryn whispered and pulled Jessica into the circle. "Look at what Kelly wore today. What's the deal with her? I wouldn't be caught dead in that!"

"What? What's wrong with what she has on?" Jessica asked as she looked at Kelly standing alone under a tree.

"She is so gross!" Kathryn said. "There's no way she's playing with us! C'mon, let's go!"

The other girls ran off. Jessica wasn't sure what to do. Kelly was her friend from church. They had been friends since the second grade. Right now Jessica wasn't sure whom to choose as her friend. It wasn't fair that she had to choose, anyway, but Kathryn was always bossing her around.

Kathryn tugged at her arm. "C'mon, I said. Let's play!"

"But Kelly's my friend too, Kathryn," Jessica said and looked over to see Kelly coming her way.

"Look! If you don't do what I say, then you're not my best friend anymore!" Kathryn demanded and ran away.

"Oh, God, help me do what's right. Help me choose Your way," Jessica prayed quietly as Kelly walked toward her. She looked to see the other girls running away from them.

"Do you want to swing?" Kelly asked Jessica. Kelly seemed not to notice Kathryn glaring at both of them.

"Yeah, let's swing," Jessica answered.

Later, when they lined up to go back into their class, Kathryn said, "You can forget about coming to my birthday party this weekend. You're not my friend anymore!"

Kathryn wouldn't talk to Jessica the rest of the day. During the last few hours of the school day, Kathryn and the other girls passed notes and whispered whenever they got the chance. Several times one of the girls looked past Jessica and pretended not to even see her. Jessica felt like she'd made the right choice, but now she wasn't sure. She could feel the tears welling up in her eyes, and a big lump was forming in her throat.

When the bell rang, Jessica grabbed her backpack and ran as fast as she could out the classroom door. Her mom was waiting for her outside.

"Jessie, what's wrong?" Mom asked. She could tell from looking at Jessica's face that she was about to cry.

"Let's go to the car, Mom, please," Jessica pleaded.

They walked in silence, and when they got to the car Jessica opened the door and dived in. She burst into tears before her mother slid in beside her from the driver's side.

Through sobs and broken sentences, she explained to her mother what had happened, the choice she had made, how she felt good afterward, but then how terrible she had felt the rest of the day. She was confused about whether she'd made the right choice.

"It'll be OK," Mom kept repeating as she stroked Jessica's hair. "It'll be OK."

When Jessica finally stopped crying, her mother started the car and took her home.

"I have something I want to show you," Mom said. She took Jessica down to her office. She pointed to a poster on her wall and read it to Jessica.

"For the eyes of the Lord are on the righteous and his ears are attentive to their prayer, but the face of the Lord is against those who do evil." Who is going to harm you if you are eager to do good? But even if you should suffer for what is right, you are blessed. "Do not fear what they fear; do not be frightened." (1 Peter 3:12–14)

After she read the poster, Mom said, "Jessica, I'm so proud of you. You made a very tough choice today. Kathryn wasn't being a good leader, and you didn't follow her. Sometimes even when we make the right choices, everything doesn't work out perfectly like a storybook ending."

"That's for sure," Jessica said.

"But, you know what, Jessie, just like this Scripture, you have to follow good leaders and do the right things anyway. Does that make sense?"

"I guess so," Jessica said. "I don't want to be like Kathryn; she's mean to people."

"Then continue to choose good leaders, and you'll be a good leader for others!" Mom said as she gave Jessica a big hug.

As Mom walked out of the office, Jessica stood and read the poster again. She was glad that God had helped her make the right choice today.

What the Story Says

Choose the right leaders,
even if it's not the popular choice.

Discussion Questions

For Both:

1. Why was Jessica not sure whom to choose as her friend?

2. Why do you think Kathryn was acting the way she was?

3. What would you have done if you had been Jessica?

4. Has anything like this ever happened to you? Tell each other about it, and write below what you did.

What Does the Bible Say?

Mom, help your daughter look up the following Scriptures and fill in the blanks.

Psalm 25:4
Show me _____ ways, O LORD, _____ me your _____.

Psalm 32:8
I will _____ you and _____ you in the way you should go; I will _____ you and _____ over you.

Isaiah 48:17
This is what the LORD says—your Redeemer, the Holy One of Israel: "I am the LORD _____ God, who _____ you what is _____ for you, who _____ you in the way you should go."

Daughter:

Who will teach us what is best for us?

_____

Mom:

What has God taught you that you discovered was best for you?

_____

Daughter:

What word is found in all three of the verses above?
T_____

How does God do this?

_____

Looking Deeper

For Both:

Take a few minutes to pray together using the verses you have just studied. Ask God to show you more about Himself. Thank God that He watches over you. Ask God to show you what you should do about a current problem you're facing.

For Mom:

Take ten minutes to play the game "Follow the Leader." First, allow your daughter to be the leader, and then it will be your turn. Have fun, and be creative. Afterward, talk about what it took to follow the leader well. Then discuss what it takes to follow Jesus well.

REMEMBER . . .
You can be a good example to your friends
by following Jesus as your leader.

For Both:

Discuss and list three ways you can follow Jesus as your leader.

1. _____

2. _____

3. _____

Great! Now you have a plan! Try practicing it this week.

We are to remember God in everything that we do. What are your plans for tomorrow? How can you remember God while you are doing these things?

Daughter:

_____

_____

Mom:

_____

_____

Check with each other at the end of tomorrow to see how it went.

Action Idea

Have a crazy hat night. Each of you create a crazy hat by only using materials or objects from around your house. Then play "Follow the Leader" once again, this time wearing your hats.

Words to Memorize

Show me your ways, O LORD, teach me your paths.
Psalm 25:4

Your Goal for This Week

_____

_____

_____

Closing Prayer

Dear Jesus, be my leader in every way. I want to follow You. Amen.

Week 7

COME TO
MY HOUSE

Scripture Reading for This Week

Romans 12:13
Share with God's people who are in need. Practice hospitality.

Hospitality means to welcome people into your home.

Mom: For this week, treat your daughter to your hospitality. Decorate the table with a nice tablecloth, napkins, and a centerpiece. Serve your daughter a special snack on your best dishes.

Daughter: Who is someone you really like to visit? Draw a picture of that person's home on the next page and talk about why you like to visit this person's home.

Mom: Whom do you know who has the gift of hospitality?

_____

What is special about this person's hospitality?

_____

It was one week before Christmas. Holly Pierce was so excited that she could hardly wait. Not only was Christmas a few days away, but her birthday was just two days after Christmas. Her parents had named her Holly because her birthday was so close to Christmas.

This would be Holly's ninth birthday, and she and her mother had already sent out the invitations for her party. This would be her first birthday party with the friends from her new school. Holly wanted everything to be perfect—just right and lots of fun!

Her sister Abbie would come home tomorrow from college for her Christmas break. Abbie had promised to help Holly decide on the games they would play and the party favors that Holly would give out to her friends.

Everyone loved Abbie, and Holly was sure her new friends would like her too. Abbie had a way of making Holly feel very special. Holly always looked forward to having Abbie home from college.

While the Pierces were having dinner that night, Mrs. Pierce mentioned Lindsay, her piano student. She said, "Lindsay's mother is going into the hospital tomorrow for surgery."

"Oh, I'm sorry to hear that," Mr. Pierce said.

"I'm concerned about where Lindsay will stay while her mother is in the hospital," Mrs. Pierce said.

Holly knew Lindsay a little, but not very well. She wasn't even sure how old Lindsay was.

"Lindsay's mom is a single parent, so she doesn't have much support right now," Mrs. Pierce continued. "They don't have any family close by either."

"That's too bad," Mr. Pierce said. "How do you think we can help?"

Oh no! Holly thought. *Don't say you're going to have her stay here! That will ruin everything!*

"Well, I was thinking that maybe she could stay with us," Mrs. Pierce said.

Yuck! Holly thought. *I guess I'll have to share my room with her too!*

Mrs. Pierce said, "I just feel that would be the right thing to do, don't you?"

"No!" Holly blurted out without even thinking. Holly's parents stared at her in disbelief. "It's almost Christmas! And we've already planned my birthday party! And Abbie's coming home! Why can't she stay somewhere else?" Holly demanded.

"Holly," Mr. Pierce said, "we always try to help people when we can."

"Our home is open to people who need it," Mrs. Pierce added.

Mr. Pierce reached over and softly patted Holly's hand. "I know how excited you've been for Christmas and your birthday. We're excited too, but think about Lindsay and her mom. It's going to be hard enough for them being away from each other at Christmastime. This is a great way for us to show God's love to Lindsay and her mom."

Mr. Pierce pulled Holly over to his lap. "Holly, why don't we pray about this and see what Jesus wants us to do?" Holly laid her head against her dad's shoulder and quietly agreed that she too would pray about it.

That evening after finishing her homework and piano practice, Holly climbed into bed. First, Holly prayed for her parents, then Abbie, then her friends. She thanked Jesus for a good day at school, and then she remembered that she had promised to pray about having Lindsay stay with them over Christmas.

"Dear Jesus, I'm not sure I want Lindsay to stay with us. It will be very different having someone here that I don't know that well for Christmas and my birthday. But, Jesus, I don't want to be selfish, and I want to share what You've given my family with others. I want to do the right thing and have a good attitude. Please help me."

The next morning on her way out the door to catch the school bus, Holly turned to her mom and said, "You and Dad were right—we should share our home with others. Do you think we can call Lindsay's mother today and invite Lindsay to stay with us? I hope she'll want to come."

Mrs. Pierce smiled. "Yes, when you get home, we can call her," she said. "Thank you for being hospitable to Lindsay, sweetie."

What the Story Says

Hospitality may be hard, but Jesus
likes us to welcome visitors.

Discussion Questions

For Daughter:

1. Holly wanted to have a good attitude, but she struggled
   to do what was right. When have you felt that way about
   sharing your home or toys with others?

   _____

   _____

2. What helped you do what was right?

   _____

   _____

3. What did Holly do to help her make the right decision?

   _____

   _____

For Mom:

1. Why did Mr. and Mrs. Pierce think it was important to
   show hospitality to Lindsay?

   _____

   _____

What Does the Bible Say?

Mom, help your daughter look up the following Scriptures and fill in the blanks.

1 Peter 4:9
Offer _____ to one _____ without _____.

What does the word "grumble" mean?

Romans 12:13
_____ with God's _____ who are in _____. _____ hospitality.

What does it mean to "practice hospitality"?

1 Timothy 5:10
And is well known for her _____ deeds, such as bringing up _____, showing _____, _____ the feet of the saints, _____ those in trouble and _____ herself to all kinds of _____ deeds.

Mom:

Tell your daughter the good hospitable deeds you've seen her perform for your family or friends. Write some of them below.

_____

_____

_____

Looking Deeper

For Both:

List two ways you can practice hospitality.

Daughter:

1. _____

2. _____

Mom:

1. _____

2. _____

For Both:

If a new family moves into your neighborhood, you could welcome them by baking a cake and taking it over to them, or you could invite them to your home for lunch or dinner.

List three ways you could show someone new that you care. Be creative with your ideas.

1. _____

2. _____

3. _____

For Mom:

Tell your daughter about a time when you practiced hospitality for others. How did that make you feel?

_____

_____

It's important that we show our daughters how we are blessed by serving others and taking the time to show that we care. And remember: Not only do you show hospitality for your Christian friends and church family; you can use hospitality as an outreach to those who don't know God.

Action Ideas

- Host a mother/daughter tea party for the girls and mothers in your daughter's class at school.
- Invite an elderly neighbor or friend from your church to your house for dessert. Have your daughter plan questions to ask your guest about his or her childhood.
- If you have a new girl in your neighborhood or class at school, have a "welcoming party" for her.

Words to Memorize

Share with God's people who are in need. Practice hospitality.
Romans 12:13

Your Goal for This Week

_____

_____

_____

Closing Prayer

Dear Jesus, help me serve others and be sensitive to their needs. Amen.

Week 8

SAYING "I'M SORRY"

Scripture Reading for This Week

Matthew 18:21–22
Then Peter came to Jesus and asked, "Lord, how many times shall I forgive my brother when he sins against me? Up to seven times?"
Jesus answered, "I tell you, not seven times, but seventy-seven times."

Daughter: How many times does Jesus say to forgive someone?

_____

Does that seem like a lot of times to you? Why or why not?

_____

Mom: Does Jesus want us to stop forgiving people when we reach seventy-seven times? Explain.

_____

Have you ever had someone in your life whom you had to forgive a lot? If so, tell your daughter about how you had to forgive
that person.

_____

_____

_____

*F*rom the first day Tracy's family arrived in their new city,
Tracy and Julie were friends. Tracy was in the third grade and
her new best friend was one year ahead in the fourth grade. They
were a little shy with each other at first, but before long they
couldn't stop talking to each other. They spent all their time
together.

Tracy and Julie attended the same school and the same
church. These two girls had a lot in common. Both were the
youngest children in their family, and they both had an older sister named Jennifer. They were good students and liked school.
Both enjoyed sports. They liked going to school activities, going
to camp, and swimming.

There was one big difference between these two girls,
though. Tracy's favorite thing to do was play basketball, and
Julie's favorite thing was to sit and read a good book.

Tracy's friendship with Julie was very important to her.
There were few times that they did not get along. When they
weren't together at each other's homes, they were talking and
laughing on the phone. It was obvious that these two girls enjoyed
spending time together.

The summer after Tracy finished fifth grade, she told Julie a
secret—something Tracy didn't want to talk about with her
other friends. Since the girls were such close friends, Tracy believed
that she could trust Julie with this special secret. Julie had always
kept her secrets before.

Later that summer, though, another friend told Tracy that

she knew her secret. Tracy rushed home to her bedroom and closed the door. She cried for hours, and there seemed to be nothing that her mother could do to help her feel better.

Later that night, Julie came by Tracy's house with a letter of apology and to ask for Tracy's forgiveness. When Tracy's mother told Tracy that Julie had come over, Tracy didn't want to talk to Julie.

"Tell her to go away," Tracy pleaded.

"Tracy, Julie is here, so I think you need to talk to her," her mother told her.

Tracy held back at first, but then she came out to talk to Julie.

"I'm sorry I told your secret," Julie said and handed Tracy a letter that she'd written. Tracy read Julie's letter asking for forgiveness. Once she finished reading the letter, Tracy held it and looked down at the floor.

Julie stood very still and waited to see if her friend would be able to forgive her. Finally, Tracy looked up and reached out to Julie. They hugged each other, and they both cried.

"I am so sorry," Julie said. "Your friendship is more important to me than anything. I shouldn't have told your secret."

"I forgive you," Tracy said. "You're still my best friend!"

That night Tracy and Julie realized that forgiveness is a very special part of friendship.

What the Story Says
Even best friends have to be able
to forgive each other at times.

Discussion Questions

For Both:

1. Why was it wrong for Julie to tell others what Tracy told her?

   _____

   _____

   _____

2. Why is it important that our friends can trust us?

   _____

   _____

   _____

3. What are some ways we can be friends who can be trusted?

   _____

   _____

   _____

4. When we do something wrong to a friend or someone in our family, why do we need to apologize and ask for the person's forgiveness?

   _____

   _____

   _____

5. When someone apologizes to us, why should we forgive the person?

_____

_____

What Does the Bible Say?

Mom, help your daughter look up the following Scriptures and fill in the blanks.

Matthew 6:14–15
For if you _____ men when they _____ against you, your heavenly _____ will also _____ you. But if you do not _____ men their sins, your Father will not _____ your sins.

What does God want us to do for others when they sin against us?

Luke 17:3–4
So watch yourselves. If your brother _____, rebuke him, and if he repents, _____ him. If he sins against you _____ times in a day, and _____ times comes back to you and says, "I repent," _____ him.

Colossians 3:13
Bear with each _____ and forgive whatever _____ you may have against one _____. Forgive as the _____ forgave you.

How has God forgiven us?

Looking Deeper

For Mom:

What was the name of your best friend when you were your daughter's age?

Did you ever experience a time with that friend where you needed to forgive her or to be forgiven by her? Tell your daughter about that time.

For Daughter:

What is the hardest thing about having to say "I'm sorry"?

For Mom:

What's the most difficult thing about forgiving someone?

For Both:

How does it help you to forgive others when you think about all that God has forgiven you?

List three ways you can help each other be more forgiving in your friendships.

1. _____

2. _____

3. _____

Think about it: Is there anyone you need to forgive? Is there anyone you need to apologize to?

Action Ideas

Talk to your daughter about how forgiveness is backward from what most people do today. Then plan a fun family night by having a "backward" dinner. Eat dessert first, then your main course, then salad, and your appetizer last. Set your table backward too—knives and spoons on the left and forks on the right. Require all your family members to come dressed for the dinner with their clothes on backward.

Celebrate each member of your family from the youngest to the oldest. Play a game where you remember things about each other, starting with the present and going back until each person's birth.

Words to Memorize

Be kind and compassionate to one another, forgiving each other,
just as in Christ God forgave you.
Ephesians 4:32

Your Goal for This Week

_____

_____

_____

Closing Prayer

Dear Jesus, please help me to forgive those who have hurt me, and help those friends I have hurt to forgive me. Amen.

Section Three

KNOWING
GOD

Week 9

BELONGING TO GOD

Scripture Reading for This Week

John 1:12
Yet to all who received him, to those who believed in his name,
he gave the right to become children of God.

Daughter: What privileges do you have in your family that girls
who aren't part of your family don't have?

_____

_____

Mom: What does it mean to be a child of God?

_____

_____

What are some privileges for the child of God?

_____

_____

*I*f I (Christine) wanted to go to church when I was eight years old, I went by myself. My parents did not go to church, but they let me go if I asked. I didn't really understand everything about church, but I knew that I liked to be there. I liked the way people treated me, and I liked to hear the stories from the Bible.

Every Sunday at the end of our class time, the teacher led our all-girl class in prayer. Almost always, we went around our circle and each person prayed one-sentence prayers. The girls would pray "thank You for the trees, thank You for the flowers, thank You for my puppy," and other prayers like that.

At the end of the prayer time, someone always said, "In Jesus' name, amen." That was one thing I didn't understand. I thought, *I'm never going to say that; I'm never going to say "In Jesus' name."* I never told anyone on earth that I had thought that—until much later.

Years went by, and I quit going to church. I became a cheerleader, played on the starting lineup of our basketball team, and was elected the president of our high school student body. I was popular and I won honors, but I still felt sad. I worked very hard on my grades—and never made anything less than an A in high school. I graduated as the top student in my senior class. I guess you could say that from the outside it looked like I had everything.

But I didn't. On the inside, I felt sad.

I went away to college, and I tried to fit in there. I did things that I should not have done. I did what I thought other people wanted me to do so they would like me. The sadness inside me seemed to grow even more.

My older sister Terryl gave me a book about a man whose life was like mine. He was different from me because he had a lot of money, he was famous, and he was very successful in his career. He was like me, though, because he still was not happy. He lost everything he owned or valued, and then he found Jesus. He gave his life to Jesus and finally lost the sadness in his heart.

That made me start thinking, because my heart felt sadder than ever. I was not very happy with my life.

I prayed to God and said, "If You're real, I want You to show me." I still had the Bible that someone had given me when I had gone to church as a child, so I started reading it.

I read Matthew, Mark, Luke, and John—all four Gospels in the New Testament. God continued to teach me about what He was like. One night while I was reading the Bible, I read John 16:24: "Until now you have not asked for anything in my name. Ask and you will receive, and your joy will be complete."

Instantly, I understood that God was real! He knew that when I was eight years old I said in my heart that I would never ask for anything in His name. God knew everything about me. He loved me and He wanted to change the sadness in my heart with His joy.

I prayed, asking Jesus to come into my life and take away my sins and my sadness. Because Jesus died on the cross for my sins, God forgave me of my sins and welcomed me into His family. And I ended my prayer "In Jesus' name."

That was more than 20 years ago. God continues to fill my life with joy and to show me what it means to belong to Him. I am so thankful that God knows everything about me and that He accepts and loves me. Every day, life is an adventure of discovering what it means to belong to God.

What the Story Says
Without Jesus, a person's life is missing something.

Discussion Questions

For Mom:

What does it mean to belong?

_____

_____

_____

For Both:

1. Name someone or something that belongs to you.

   Mother: _____

   Daughter: _____

2. Have a "Show 'n' Tell" time. On "go," each of you race to your room or anywhere else in your house to find the three most special things that belong to you. Race back to your meeting area. Then tell each other why these things are special to you and why you're glad they belong to you.

   Mother, write down what each of you chose, and why.

   I chose_____

   because _____

   _____.

   My daughter chose _____

   because _____

   _____.

3. How do you treat someone or something special that belongs to you?

_____

_____

_____

4. How does it make you feel when you belong to someone?

_____

_____

_____

What Does the Bible Say?

Mom, help your daughter look up the following Scriptures and fill in the blanks.

John 8:47
He who _____ to God _____ what God says. The _____ you do not hear is that you do not _____ to God.

Romans 1:6
And _____ also are among those who are _____ to _____ to _____ _____.

Acts 4:12
_____ is found in _____ one else, for there is no other _____ under heaven _____ to men by which we must be _____.

Romans 10:9–10
That if you _____ with your _____, "Jesus is

_____," and _____ in your heart that God _____ him from the dead, you will be _____. For it is with your _____ that you _____ and are justified, and it is with your mouth that you _____ and are _____.

Looking Deeper

For Both:

Why does belonging to God bring happiness?

_____

_____

_____

Name two reasons it's important that we belong to God.

Daughter:

1. _____

2. _____

Mother:

1. _____

2. _____

For Mom:

Tell your daughter one reason you're happy she belongs to you.

_____

_____

For Daughter:

Tell your mom one reason you're happy she belongs to you.

_____

_____

How I Know I Belong to God

God loves you and wants you to love Him too. When God made the world, He gave the first man and woman a rule to obey. But Adam and Eve chose to disobey God rather than obey. They made a bad choice, and they broke God's rule.

Because Adam and Eve sinned, they caused a separation between themselves and God. All of Adam and Eve's children and grandchildren were separated from God forever. Even though Adam and Eve broke God's rule, God still loved them. And God still loves us even if we break His rules.

God loves us so much that He sent His Son Jesus to take the punishment for our sins. We deserved to be punished, but Jesus was punished for us instead. If we accept Jesus' gift of forgiveness, we can become part of God's family and live with God forever. You belong to God if you have accepted Jesus' gift of forgiveness and eternal life.

If you belong to God's family, God has given you a very special helper named the Holy Spirit. The Holy Spirit will live with you and guide you. Because you belong to God, you will live with God forever in heaven when you die.

Action Idea

Make a special dessert that has been in your family for ages. Talk about the different ingredients that go into the dessert to make it taste good (even if some of the ingredients don't taste good by themselves). Talk about how everyone in your family is necessary to make your family (or your church) just the way it is—like all the ingredients are necessary to make your dessert. Then afterward, tell your family how much you love and care for them and how happy you are to be a part of the same family.

Words to Memorize

The Spirit himself testifies with our spirit
that we are God's children.
Romans 8:16

Your Goal for This Week

_____

_____

_____

Closing Prayer

Dear Jesus, thank You that Your Word has shown us that we can become Your children and be a part of Your family. Amen.

Week 10

TALKING TO GOD

Scripture Reading for This Week

Philippians 4:6
Do not be anxious about anything, but in everything, by prayer and petition, with thanksgiving, present your requests to God.

Someone once said that God answers every prayer. He may answer yes, no, or wait.

Mother and Daughter: What does this verse say?

_____

_____

*W*hen Hope Smith was eight years old, she studied Mongolia for a homeschool project. As part of her research, she learned about Buddhism, the biggest religion of Mongolia. Almost every home has a Buddhist shrine or altar where people worship. Hope also learned that there are very few Christians in Mongolia.

So after she wrote her school report, Hope began to pray for the people in Mongolia. Hope prayed that God would replace the Buddhist altars in their homes with Bibles.

Two years after her first prayer for the people of Mongolia, Hope read in a missions magazine that God had started answering her prayers. More than 500 people had accepted Christ as their Savior in Mongolia. The article was titled "Hope for Mongolia," and Hope believed that God was telling her that He was answering her prayers.

Hope continued to pray. The 500 Christians witnessed to other people, and soon there were 1,000 Christians. Their first church was going to be named "Hope Assembly."

Many churches honored Hope for her part in asking God to do amazing things in Mongolia. But even more important than that, Hope knows that God used her prayers to change the world. God wants to use your prayers to change the world too.

What the Story Says
God listens to our prayers and answers them.

Discussion Questions

For Mom:

Tell about a time that you prayed for something and God answered your prayer.

_____

_____

For Daughter:

Tell about a time that you prayed for something and God answered your prayer.

_____

_____

For Mom:

1. When is a time that you prayed for something and God said no to your request? How did you see God's protection in not giving you what you wanted?

   _____

   _____

2. Tell your daughter something that you've prayed for her that God has already answered.

   _____

   _____

3. Tell your daughter something that you're praying for her that God may not answer until the future (such as for her husband).

   _____

   _____

Tell each other personal prayer requests that you would like each other to continually pray about. Write a few below.

_____

_____

What Does the Bible Say?

Mom, help your daughter look up the following Scriptures and fill in the blanks.

Psalm 54:2
Hear my _____, O God; _____ to the _____ of my mouth.

Luke 11:9–10
So I say to you: _____ and it will be _____ to you; _____ and you will _____; _____ and the door will be _____ to you. For _____ who asks _____; he who seeks _____; and to him who _____, the door will be _____.

Colossians 4:2
_____ yourselves to _____, being _____ and _____.

Looking Deeper

Read Luke 11:5–8.
Why did the man finally get up and give his friend the bread?

_____

_____

Read Luke 11:9–10.
What does this Scripture show about prayer?

_____

_____

This Scripture holds a powerful promise about prayer. Stop right now and together thank God for the amazing gift of prayer that He has given us.

Read Luke 11:11–13.
What kind of father gives his children bad things when they ask for gifts?

_____

_____

What did Jesus think of this kind of father?

_____

_____

What kind of father does Jesus say our heavenly Father is?

_____

_____

What does this teach us about talking to God?

_____

_____

Action Ideas

- Make prayer journals. For each journal, you'll need a bright-colored sheet of card stock and several sheets of typing paper. Fold the card stock, with the narrow edges touching. Crease the fold.

  Insert the typing paper into the card stock and fold again to make a book. Punch three holes along the folded edge of your book and through all the sheets of paper. Attach a paper fastener through each hole to keep your book together. Then decorate the cover of your journal.

  Work together to create personal prayer lists in your journals. Make two columns on each sheet of paper. Down the left-hand column, write the date and the prayer request. Then as God answers each prayer, write the answer and the date in the right-hand column. Update your prayer journals regularly.

- If you've been praying for someone in your family, a friend, or a neighbor, write that person a note or send a card about how you've been praying. The person will be encouraged and thankful that someone cares enough to pray for him or her.

Words to Memorize

So I say to you: Ask and it will be given to you; seek and you will find; knock and the door will be opened to you.
Luke 11:9

Your Goal for This Week

_____

_____

_____

Closing Prayer

Dear Jesus, thank You for listening to my prayers and never tiring of hearing me talk to You. Amen.

Week 11

LISTENING TO GOD

Scripture Reading for This Week

Psalm 1:1–4
Blessed is the man who does not walk in the counsel of the wicked or stand in the way of sinners or sit in the seat of mockers. But his delight is in the law of the LORD, and on his law he meditates day and night. He is like a tree planted by streams of water, which yields its fruit in season and whose leaf does not wither. Whatever he does prospers. Not so the wicked! They are like chaff that the wind blows away.

Daughter: Tell about your favorite tree. Why do you like it?

_____

_____

_____

Mom: Tell about a favorite tree from your childhood. Why did you like it?

_____

_____

*P*aul and Mary Scott quietly serve in many ways in their church. And they've served Jesus for more than 40 years. So many things in their church would never happen as smoothly as they do if it weren't for the Scotts' behind-the-scenes service.

A normal week for the Scotts is filled with a Bible study in their home, planning meetings for the children's church program, baking and decorating cakes for people's parties, praying with and talking to hurting people, taking care of an elderly uncle on Saturday mornings, and then showing up on Sunday mornings to greet and serve children.

The children in their church know that the Scotts will always be there for them. Mary greets each child by name, and Paul pats the little children on the back and teases them to get a good smile out of them. They really want to know the children.

If a kid gets too rowdy in class and can't settle down, the kid is sent to spend time with the Scotts in the office. Paul and Mary will ask that child what is going on. They encourage the child to remember the rules, and then they pray with the child.

Paul and Mary Scott remind me a lot of a strong towering tree that gives shade and comfort to the people who sit under its branches. They are able to help so many people because they listen to what the Bible says. We could say that their lives are deeply rooted in God's Word. They spend time daily with God and pray to God about every concern they have. When other people are worried about something, Mr. and Mrs. Scott encourage them to trust God because He has always taken care of us.

Paul and Mary Scott are like the tree talked about in Psalm 1, because they delight in God's Word and meditate on it day and night. They have strong roots into God's love and His Word.

Trees have to have strong roots to protect them against the strong winds that can blow against them. If a tree doesn't have strong roots, it can be blown over easily. It takes a tree years and years to grow tall and strong. Trees also need healthy roots to give them nourishment from the soil and water. Without good roots, a tree would starve to death. And without knowing what the Bible says, a Christian won't know how to obey God.

What the Story Says

Strong Christians trust the Bible the way
a strong tree depends on its roots.

Discussion Questions

For Mom:

Why do you think Paul and Mary have been able to serve God for so many years?

_____

_____

_____

For Daughter:

What does a tree need to help it grow to be big and strong?

_____

Draw a picture of a tree. List beside the roots of the tree what God wants to use to help us grow strong. Write on the tree's branches words that show the kind of fruit that a strong Christian will have in his or her life. (See Galatians 5:22–23.)

What Does the Bible Say?

Mom, help your daughter look up the following Scriptures and fill in the blanks.

1 Peter 2:2
Like _____ babies, crave _____ spiritual _____, so that by it you may _____ up in your _____.

2 Peter 3:18
But _____ in the _____ and _____ of our _____ and _____ Jesus Christ. To him be _____ both now and _____! Amen.

Colossians 2:6–7
So then, just as you _____ Christ _____ as _____, continue to _____ in _____, rooted and _____ up in him, _____ in the _____ as you were _____, and _____ with _____.

Looking Deeper

For Daughter:

Trees get water and nourishment through their roots. But a baby needs milk. Why does a baby need milk?

_____

_____

_____

_____

For Mom:

What does 1 Peter 2:2 mean when it talks about milk? What kind of spiritual milk do we need so we can grow as Christians?

_____

_____

_____

For Both:

If you were a tree, what kind of tree would you want to be, and why?

_____

_____

_____

For Daughter:

What do a tree's roots do?

_____

_____

_____

For Mom:

What does it mean to be rooted in Jesus?

_____

_____

_____

For Both:

How can we listen to God?

_____

_____

_____

For Daughter:

How have you grown in your relationship with Jesus as you and your mother have been doing this study together?

_____

_____

_____

For Mom:

What helps you grow in your relationship with Jesus?

_____

_____

_____

For Daughter:

What questions do you have for your mother about growing in your relationship with Jesus?

_____

_____

_____

Take turns praying for each other to be rooted and established in God's Word so you can grow to be strong in Jesus.

Action Ideas

- Invite a long-time Christian in your church to lunch or dinner. Interview this person to find out what he or she has done to grow strong in the Lord.
- Plant a tree in your backyard. Together, pray that God will help your tree take good root and grow strong. Then pray for each other that God will help each of you grow strong as Christians.

Words to Memorize

Do not merely listen to the word, and so deceive yourselves.
Do what it says.
James 1:22

Your Goal for This Week

_____

_____

_____

Closing Prayer

Dear Jesus, help me to listen to Your Word and to grow in it every day so I can be strong in You.

Week 12

TELLING OTHERS ABOUT JESUS

Scripture Reading for This Week

Matthew 5:14–16
You are the light of the world. A city on a hill cannot be hidden. Neither do people light a lamp and put it under a bowl. Instead they put it on its stand, and it gives light to everyone in the house. In the same way, let your light shine before men, that they may see your good deeds and praise your Father in heaven.

Daughter: What does a light do for us? _____

Mom: How does a light work? _____

Sing "This Little Light of Mine" together, and then talk about how you can let your light shine for Jesus.

Nine-year-old Katie Chambers is in the fourth grade. She loves to read. She especially likes the Nancy Drew series. Katie also enjoys playing the piano and has just started her fourth year of piano lessons. One of Katie's favorite things to do is play with her younger sister, Mary, and brother, Chip.

People love to be Katie's friends because Katie is so easy to talk to. She's also a lot of fun to be with. Katie makes friends easily because she cares about people. Most of all, Katie cares about whether people know Jesus or not. Katie wants to tell others about Jesus and His love and care for them.

One winter, Katie asked her parents if she could play on a softball team in the spring. She hoped that she would be on the same team as her friend Laurel. Katie was excited to try something new.

After Katie's parents signed her up for the league, Katie found out that Laurel was not on her team, and she did not know any of the girls on her team. Katie was a little nervous about playing with girls she didn't know, but she remembered that she had been wanting to make some new friends.

On the first night of practice, Katie and her dad arrived a little early. The only other girl there was sitting behind the dugout with her mom. Katie could tell that the girl was shy, so she walked over to her.

"Hi! My name is Katie," she said. "Are you on the Summerfield Nightmares team too?"

"Yes," said the girl shyly. "My name is Ashley."

"Have you ever played softball before?" Katie asked.

"No, it's my first time," Ashley said.

"Mine too!" Katie said with a laugh. "So I guess we'll have to learn together."

The girls hit it off from the start.

One day at practice, Katie and Ashley talked and laughed as they tossed the ball back and forth to each other.

"Hey, Ashley," Katie asked, "do you go to church?"

"Not really," Ashley answered.

"Do you want to come to church with me?" Katie asked.

"Sure!" Ashley answered quickly.

"Can you come over to my house today?" Katie asked.

"Let me ask my mom," Ashley said.

After checking with Ashley's mom, the two girls loaded into the Chamberses' car. The girls had a great time at Katie's house —they stayed inside to cool off after their game and watched a "Veggie Tales" video because Ashley had never seen one before.

Then they headed up to Katie's bedroom to play. As the girls sat on Katie's bed, Katie asked, "Ashley, do you know what it means to be a Christian?"

"I don't think so," Ashley answered.

They talked about heaven and what it meant to know God. Katie could tell by some of Ashley's answers that she didn't understand everything. Katie remembered her talks with her mom and how Mom had so carefully told Katie how she could become a Christian. Katie explained to Ashley just as her mother had explained to her.

"You know, God is perfect," Katie said. "He doesn't do anything wrong, but we do."

"Not me!" Ashley joked.

"Yeah, even you!" Katie laughed and gave Ashley a playful shove.

"Anyway," Katie said and rolled her eyes in mock frustration, "since we're not perfect, we can't be close to God. But don't worry; God took care of that problem."

"What problem?" Ashley asked innocently.

"The problem about not being able to be near God. That's a problem because that means when we die, we won't be able to go to heaven."

"That is a problem," said Ashley.

"Well, God took care of the problem by sending Jesus to die for us. When Jesus died for us, He made it possible for us to be forgiven for all our sins," Katie explained.

"You mean like lying and stealing?" Ashley asked.

"Yeah, and every sin," Katie said.

Katie got out her Bible and showed Ashley verses to help her better understand what it meant to become a Christian. She showed Ashley John 3:16 about God's great love for each of us and His desire for each of us to know Him as our Savior.

"Do you think you'd like to become a Christian?" Katie asked.

"I don't think I'm ready yet," Ashley said.

"That's OK," Katie said, "but if you have any questions later, just let me know." Katie knew if she didn't have the answers, she could always ask her mother.

Katie and Ashley became good friends. They continued to spend time together, and they enjoyed being on the Summerfield Nightmares team. At the end of their season, as the two girls walked out to the field for practice, Ashley said, "Katie, I want to tell you something."

"OK."

"One night when I was alone in my bedroom, I asked Jesus to forgive me. I told Him that I wanted to be a Christian and follow Him," Ashley said.

Ashley could barely finish what she was saying. Katie jumped up and down in excitement. Katie knew that Ashley had made the most important decision she would ever make.

The next Sunday, Ashley, her mother, and her younger brother went to church with the Chambers. Who knows—maybe at some point Ashley's whole family may become Christians because of Katie Chambers's love for Jesus and her desire to talk with her friends about His love. The Summerfield Nightmares won most of their games and even received a trophy at the end of the season, but more important to Katie was that her new friend Ashley had accepted Jesus' special gift of forgiveness and eternal life.

What the Story Says

Telling a friend about Jesus is a good
way to show you care about her.

Discussion Questions

For Both:

Do you enjoy making new friends? Why or why not?

_____

_____

_____

For Mom:

Discuss some ideas that might make meeting new friends and trying new situations a little easier.

_____

_____

_____

For Both:

Is there something new you would like to try?

_____

_____

_____

Why was it important to Katie to tell Ashley about Jesus?

_____

_____

_____

What Does the Bible Say?

Mom, help your daughter look up the following Scriptures and fill in the blanks.

John 3:16
For _____ so _____ the world that he gave his _____ and _____ Son, that _____ believes in him shall not _____ but have _____ life.

What does "perish" mean?

_____

_____

Mark 16:15
He said to them, "_____ into _____ the _____ and preach the _____ _____ to all creation."

What is the good news?

_____

_____

Philemon 6
I pray that _____ may be _____ in _____ your _____, so that you will have a full _____ of every good thing we have in Christ.

Looking Deeper

For Daughter:

Do you want to talk about Jesus with your friends who may not know Him? Why or why not?

_____

_____

_____

List two reasons for us to tell others about Jesus' love for them:

1. _____

2. _____

Is it easy or difficult for you to talk about Jesus with your friends? Explain.

_____

_____

_____

For Both:

Name three people you would like to see become Christians. Pray that God will use you in their lives.

Daughter	*Mother*
1. _____	1. _____
2. _____	2. _____
3. _____	3. _____

For Both:

Looking back to the Scripture for the week, Matthew 5:14–16, list ways you can be a light to your friends who don't know Jesus.

_____

_____

_____

Action Ideas

- Tape a large sheet of paper to a window or a doorway, at the level of your daughter's head. Have your daughter stand behind the paper, with one side of her face toward you. Turn off the lights. Then shine a flashlight on your daughter's face. Prop up the flashlight and lightly draw your daughter's silhouette onto the paper. Place your drawing on a table and make the lines darker.

  Have your daughter do the same for you as you sit in a chair. Afterward, talk about how the light helped you see things that you wouldn't have seen in the dark.

- Together, commit to pray for the people you listed earlier who need to know about Jesus' love. Pray for these people every day this month. Ask God to give you opportunities to tell them about Jesus' love.

- Write a letter to a non-Christian friend and tell your friend about Jesus' love. Explain how you decided to follow Jesus and accept His forgiveness. You can send the letter to your friend or keep it. Either way, this will help make it easier for you to find the words to tell a friend about your relationship with Jesus.

Words to Memorize

Jesus answered, "I am the way and the truth and the life.
No one comes to the Father except through me."
John 14:6

Your Goal for This Week

_____

_____

_____

Closing Prayer

Dear Jesus, thank You for loving us. Help us to discuss Your love
with people who don't know You.

Section Four

DOING WHAT'S RIGHT

Week 13

TELLING THE TRUTH

Scripture Reading for This Week

Psalm 25:4–5
Show me your ways, O LORD, teach me your paths; guide me in your truth and teach me, for you are God my Savior, and my hope is in you all day long.

Both: What was the writer of this psalm asking God to help him do?

_____

_____

_____

Why is it important to stay on God's path?

_____

_____

_____

*W*hen I (Donna) was a young girl, I loved to visit my cousin Jennifer. We lived far apart. I lived in Missouri and she lived in upstate New York. That's one thousand miles apart! Usually I was only able to visit Jennifer during our summer vacation because she lived so far away.

Jennifer and I had a lot in common. We were both the youngest in our families. We both had only sisters—no brothers! School was important to both of us. And we both loved sports. In fact, we both were always open to playing any kind of game.

Even though we were alike in so many ways, we were also different from each other. Jennifer lived on 200 acres of land, but I lived in a city. Jennifer had a beautiful Morgan horse, but before I visited her for the first time I had never even ridden a horse. Jennifer had traveled to many different countries with her parents on mission trips. I had never been outside of the United States.

I admired and looked up to Jennifer for many reasons. For one thing, she was a whole year older than I was, and she seemed to know so much about all kinds of things. Jennifer was also very willing to try new things. She always seemed excited to try a new challenge.

Another difference I noticed in Jennifer was how she wanted to obey her parents and she talked kindly to them. That wasn't always easy for me, but Jennifer was a great example for me in that area. Jennifer was also a very honest and truthful person. I could tell she wanted to do the right thing in every situation. It was obvious to me that Jennifer loved Jesus and wanted to be like Him in every way.

In fact, I can remember an afternoon during one of my visits to Jennifer's house when Aunt Virginia had taken us to church for a youth day. After we played volleyball for hours at church, Jennifer and I walked to an ice cream shop. It was right around the corner from the church, and Aunt Virginia had said that it would be OK for us to go there. I remember feeling older because we were there on our own.

After finishing our ice cream, we walked up to the owner to pay. As we were about to walk out the door, Jennifer noticed something. She looked at me and told me she needed to go back to return some money. The man had made a mistake and given her too much change.

When we left, I asked Jennifer, "Why did you do that?"

"Because he gave me too much money," she answered.

"But why did you give it back?" I asked.

"Because it was the honest thing to do," Jennifer explained. "And that's what Jesus would have wanted me to do."

Even thirty years later I haven't forgotten Jennifer's example of obeying Jesus and being honest. That man never said thank you or even smiled at Jennifer when she gave him his money back. But that's not what mattered. Jennifer taught me to do the right thing—the thing that Jesus would want us to do. I am thankful for my cousin Jennifer's desire to be honest and truthful.

What the Story Says
Honesty is the right choice.

Discussion Questions

For Both:

1. What were some of the reasons Donna admired her cousin Jennifer so much?

   _____

   _____

   _____

2. There will be times in your life when your honesty will not be recognized. Why is it still very important to be honest in every situation?

_____

_____

_____

3. When do you find it hardest to be honest?

_____

_____

_____

4. Read Philippians 4:13.

   This verse says that we can do all things through Jesus because He gives us the strength or power to do the right thing. How can Jesus help us tell the truth?

_____

_____

_____

For Mom:

Pray right now for your daughter—that she will allow Jesus to develop her in the area of honesty.

What Does the Bible Say?

Mom, help your daughter look up the following Scriptures and fill in the blanks.

Psalm 86:11
Teach me _____ way, O LORD, and I will _____ in your
_____; give me an undivided _____, that I may fear
_____ name.

Mom, explain what this verse means by "undivided heart."

Psalm 25:5
_____ me in your _____ and _____ me, for you
are God my _____, and my _____ is in you all
day long.

Psalm 119:30
I have _____ the way of _____; I have set my
_____ on your _____.

Proverbs 20:11
Even a child is known by his _____, by whether his
_____ is pure and _____.

Looking Deeper

For Mom:

Have you had someone you admired in your life? Tell about this
person.

_____

_____

_____

For Daughter:

Have you noticed someone's honesty? (It may be a friend or
someone in your family.) As you have seen this person do or say

the right thing, how has that made you feel?

_____

_____

_____

For Mom:

Tell your daughter how her life can be an example to friends and family. She too could positively influence others as Jennifer influenced Donna's life.

_____

_____

_____

For Daughter:

List three positive things about being honest.

1. _____

2. _____

3. _____

For Mom:

List three negative things about being dishonest.

1. _____

2. _____

3. _____

Action Ideas

- For Mom: On a hand mirror, use fingernail polish or a permanent marker to write the words "Reflection of Jesus." Explain to your daughter that when people look at her, they see the reflection of Jesus; it's as though people are looking at a mirror image of Jesus. Encourage your daughter to reflect Jesus in situations that require honesty by choosing to do the right thing.

Donna's "Jennifer" is still a very lovely Christian and a doctor. Where is your "Jennifer" now? Write a letter to your "Jennifer," thanking her for the example she gave you.

- For Both: Spend quiet time with God. On separate sheets of paper, write any lie or lies that you've told and haven't confessed to God. (You don't have to show each other these sheets.) After writing these, silently talk to God and ask for forgiveness. If the lies have been to each other, this would be a good time to admit them, confess, and forgive each other.

Then use a big marker to write the words from 1 John 1:9 over the lies you've written. Thank God for His forgiveness. Tear the papers into tiny pieces and throw them into a trash can. Commit yourselves to God to speak the truth with His help even when it's difficult.

Words to Memorize

I have chosen the way of truth; I have set my heart on your laws.
Psalm 119:30

Your Goal for This Week

_____

_____

_____

Closing Prayer

Dear Jesus, help me to be honest and truthful in everything. I want to choose the way of truth.

Week 14

KINDNESS COUNTS

Scripture Reading for This Week

Galatians 6:2
Carry each other's burdens, and in this way you will fulfill the law of Christ.

A burden is something heavy. Often when we say "burden," we mean a problem that makes us sad.

Mom and Daughter: What kinds of burden have you had?

_____

_____

Mom: Tell about a time that someone helped you carry a burden.

_____

_____

Daughter: Tell about a time that someone helped you carry a burden.

_____

_____

*O*ne of my favorite animals is usually seen at places like Sea World. This animal is so fun to watch as it jumps out of the water through hoops in the air and seems to dance on its back fin.

Of course, you have probably already guessed that I am talking about dolphins. The most well-known dolphin is the bottlenose dolphin. It is the kind that is used most often in marine parks. This is the dolphin most frequently seen along the shores of the United States. Also, if a dolphin is used in a movie, it is probably a bottlenose dolphin.

This dolphin usually has a short and stubby beak that looks like the nipple on a bottle. Its upper body is colored light gray, and its belly is pale, pinkish gray. Its belly and lower sides are sometimes spotted.

An adult bottlenose dolphin can eat 15 to 30 pounds of food each day. These dolphins eat a variety of food, including fish, squid, and crustaceans (animals like lobsters and shrimp). Dolphins are mammals, so they give birth to live babies called calves. Dolphin calves drink milk from their mothers for a year or a year and a half, and they stay with their mothers for up to three years. In their time with their mothers they learn how to catch fish and do other important dolphin tasks.

Bottlenose dolphins travel in groups of about 20 if they are close to the shore. If the group is farther out at sea, there can be as many as two or three hundred dolphins in their group. Dolphins like to be around other dolphins; that is why they like to travel together. Dolphins are also playful animals.

Bottlenose dolphins die for different reasons. Some are accidentally caught in fishing gear. Bottlenose dolphins can also become sick from pollution in the water. More often, though, dolphins die because they get a disease or they're eaten by sharks or killer whales.

If a dolphin becomes diseased and dies, its closest family members become so sad that it's difficult for them to swim to the surface for air. If a dolphin doesn't move to the surface of the water for air, it can die.

Rather than let the sad dolphin die, the other dolphins will swim under it and lift it to the surface so it can breathe. The dolphins will do this until the dolphin is able to lift itself up on its own.

In many ways, other people at church remind me of these dolphins. When loved ones die, church members comfort the family members who are left behind by bringing meals and praying for them. When someone is sick, church members visit that person in the hospital. In our church, when a single mother has trouble with her car, some of our church members fix it for free.

Dolphins and faithful church members remind us to help one another carry burdens that are too heavy for us to carry on our own.

What the Story Says
It is good to help other people.

Discussion Questions

For Both:

1. Name different ways that your church members help people through their difficult times.

_____

_____

_____

2. Which of these things could the two of you do together
for someone in need?

_____

_____

_____

For Mom:

Why is it important that we help carry each other's burdens?

_____

_____

_____

For Both:

When you have helped someone during a difficult time, how has
it made you feel?

_____

_____

_____

What Does the Bible Say?

Mom, help your daughter look up the following Scriptures and
fill in the blanks.

Jeremiah 9:23–24
This is what the _____ says: "Let not the wise man boast
of his _____ or the strong man boast of his
_____ or the rich man boast of his _____,
but let him who _____ boast about this: that he

_____ and _____ me, that I am the LORD,
who exercises _____, _____ and _____
on earth, for in these I _____," declares the LORD.

*From this Scripture, what is important to God that people
should boast (brag) about?* _____
*What is not important to God that people should not boast
about?* _____

Jeremiah 31:3
The _____ appeared to us in the past, saying: "I have
_____ you with an _____ love; I have
_____ you with _____."

What does God say that He has used to draw us to Himself?
_____

Proverbs 12:25
An _____ heart _____ a man down, but a
_____ word _____ him up.

How does kindness help people carry their burdens?

Looking Deeper

For Mom:

Did you ever experience a time that someone changed your life
by being kind? Tell your daughter about that time, and write
about it below.

_____

_____

_____

For Daughter:

What's the most difficult thing about being kind to others?

_____

_____

For Both:

Why do you think God wants us to be kind to others?

_____

_____

List three ways you can help each other be kind to others.

1. _____

2. _____

3. _____

Action Idea

Ask God to show you someone in your church who is carrying a heavy burden. It may be someone who's just had a baby and needs help. Or it may be someone who is grieving the death of a loved one. Together, plan how you'll show kindness to help that person carry his or her burden. Then do it.

Words to Memorize

Make sure that nobody pays back wrong for wrong, but always try to be kind to each other and to everyone else.
1 Thessalonians 5:15

Your Goal for This Week

_____

_____

_____

Closing Prayer

Dear Jesus, help us show kindness to everyone—but especially to people who are burdened by heavy problems.

Week 15

"BECAUSE, I SAID SO!"

Scripture Reading for This Week

Romans 16:19
Everyone has heard about your obedience, so I am full of joy over you; but I want you to be wise about what is good, and innocent about what is evil.

Mom and Daughter: The apostle Paul wrote this letter to the church in Rome. Why do you think it made Paul happy to hear about the Christians in Rome obeying God?

_____

_____

_____

How does it make you feel when you see each other obey God?

_____

$\mathcal{I}$(Christine) was eight when I watched my sister, Terryl, and her friend Judy demonstrate how to make chocolate chip cookies at a 4-H contest. Terryl and Judy had practiced their speech and the steps to make cookies so they could win the cooking competition. They felt confident in their demonstration.

The day of the competition, they took turns explaining each step. They poured and stirred as they talked. Soon the demonstration was close to its end. They had added the final ingredient—chocolate chips.

Then my sister looked down at the mixing bowl. Her mouth dropped open when she saw two eggs lying on the table. There was no way to add the eggs now. Terryl and Judy looked at each other in horror. Then they looked at the competition's judge, who had also seen the eggs. They didn't win the competition, but they learned a valuable lesson about the importance of following a recipe.

It's not fair to tell you this story without telling one of my baking catastrophes. I was in high school when I needed to bake something for a bake sale. I had waited until the last minute, so I ran to the store and bought a tube of brownie dough.

I had never used this kind of cookie dough before, but it looked easy and quick. Those were the two things that were the most important to me at that time—easy and quick.

I rushed home to bake the brownies. I checked the package to see what temperature to preheat the oven—375 degrees. OK, done. I pulled out a baking pan and then dug around in the drawer for a sharp knife. Very carefully, I sliced open the plastic packaging and removed it from the tube of brownie dough.

I plopped the tube in the center of the baking pan and then slid it into the oven. I checked the time and noted when I should remove the brownies from the oven. But I didn't notice that the directions also said to spread the brownies out in the pan.

In the middle of the baking time, I checked on the brownies and couldn't believe my eyes. Rather than melting to fill the pan as I had hoped, the dough was a brown mound with melted edges.

I pulled out the pan and attacked the dough with a spatula to spread it throughout the pan. I slid the pan back into the oven and waited.

It was too late. My brownies became crumblies. There was no way I could sell those brownies at a bake sale. Sadly, in my hurry to bake the brownies, I did not read the directions, and I paid for it in the end.

Following Jesus is a lot like baking. The Bible is God's recipe for our lives. God knows the right ingredients that He wants to add to our lives and the order in which they should be added. If we want to have the very best lives, we need to read God's Word and obey every step of God's recipe for our lives.

What the Story Says

Recipes give directions for baking,
and God's Word gives directions for life.

Discussion Questions

For Mom:

Tell about a time that you failed to follow a recipe completely. What happened?

_____

_____

_____

For Daughter:

Why is it important to follow a recipe when cooking?

_____

_____

_____

For Both:

Tell about a time that you followed God's recipe for life and had a good outcome.

_____

_____

_____

What Does the Bible Say?

Mom, help your daughter look up the following Scriptures and fill in the blanks.

Jeremiah 7:23

_____ me, and I will be your _____ and you will be my _____. _____ in all the ways I _____ you, that it may go _____ with you.

John 14:15

If you _____ me, you will _____ what I _____.

1 John 5:3
This is _____ for God: to _____ his _____.
And his _____ are not _____.

Looking Deeper

Read Psalm 119:55–60.
In the night I remember your name, O LORD, and I will keep your law. This has been my practice: I obey your precepts. You are my portion, O LORD; I have promised to obey your words.I have sought your face with all my heart; be gracious to me according to your promise. I have considered my ways and have turned my steps to your statutes. I will hasten and not delay to obey your commands.

For Mom:

The easiest of the words the psalmist uses to describe God's laws is probably "commands." Explain to your daughter that "precepts" and "statutes" mean the commands or the things that God has told us to do in His Word.

For Daughter:

Does it seem like the person who wrote this passage from Scripture enjoyed obeying God? Which words can you point out that prove your answer?

_____

_____

For Mom:

What does it mean to "seek God's face with all your heart"?

_____

_____

How do you seek God's face with all your heart?

_____

_____

For Daughter:

Do you want to obey God with all your heart? Why?

_____

_____

For Both:

How can you help each other "turn your steps" to obey God's Word?

_____

_____

Action Ideas

- Choose a recipe to bake together. As you add each ingredient, discuss what would happen if that ingredient were left out of the dish. Tell your daughter what you consider to be the most important ingredients that you hope she'll add to her life with God's help.

- Draw a large Olympic medal for "winning obedience" on a sheet of paper. Make a dozen photocopies of your medal (on gold paper, if possible). Whenever you see each other obeying God when it isn't easy, celebrate by awarding each other with one of the Olympic medals. You could even choose a theme song to play, sing, or hum during your award ceremony.

Words to Memorize

We know that we have come to know
him if we obey his commands.
1 John 2:3

Your Goal for This Week

_____

_____

_____

Closing Prayer

Dear Jesus, we love You and want to do what You say. Help us to turn from anything that keeps us from obeying You with all our hearts.

Week 16

A GIFT FROM MOM'S HEART

 om and daughter, this week is your chance to
personalize your time together. First of all, Mom,
you'll start by telling your daughter a story of
your own. It could be how you came to know
Christ. It could be the story of how you met and fell in love with
your husband or some other special day in your life.

Stop and ask yourself what is the one thing you want your
daughter to know that was not covered so far in this book. If you
could tell her only one thing, what would it be?

This is your chapter.

We have provided space for you to write this story as a gift
of love for your daughter. Don't worry; it's not really important
whether it's well written—the main thing is that the story you
tell is personal. One day your daughter will treasure this simple
and meaningful portrait of her family.

Ahead of time, write the story in the book. Then when you
meet, begin by reading it aloud to her. You may prefer to "wing
it" and tell your story impromptu. Do what makes you feel the
most comfortable. But be sure you write it down at some point

so she'll have something to reread.

Then during the discussion phase of your time together, develop your own discussion questions and discuss your favorite Scripture verses.

This is a gift of love to your daughter. So get ready to tear off a piece of your heart and share it with her.

_____

_____

_____

_____

_____

_____

_____

_____

_____

_____

_____

_____

_____

_____

_____

_____

_____

_____

Week 16: A Gift from Mom's Heart

_____

_____

_____

_____

_____

_____

_____

_____

_____

_____

_____

_____

_____

_____

_____

_____

_____

_____

_____

_____

_____

_____

_____

_____

_____

_____

_____

_____

_____

_____

_____

_____

_____

_____

_____

_____

_____

_____

_____

_____

_____

_____

_____

_____

_____

_____

_____

_____

_____

_____

_____

_____

_____

_____

_____

_____

_____

_____

_____

_____

_____

_____

_____

_____

_____

_____

_____

_____

_____

_____

What Your Story Says

_____

_____

_____

Discussion Questions

1. _____

_____

2. _____

_____

3. _____

_____

What Does the Bible Say?

For Mom:

Read your favorite Scripture passages. List the references below, then help your daughter look them up and ask her to read them.

_____

_____

_____

_____

_____

_____

_____

_____

_____

Looking Deeper

Tell your daughter what you would like her to remember most
about your story. Then write it below.

_____

_____

_____

_____

_____

_____

_____

_____

_____

Action Ideas

For Mom:

This is your week, Mom. Maybe you could plan a nice tea or a special dinner for yourself and your daughter. Use your best china and candles. You may want to plan a picnic in the park or a dinner out at a nice restaurant for a special evening together. You could also have flowers, a balloon bouquet, or a cookie bouquet delivered to your house for your daughter from you.

For Daughter:

Write down what you did with your mother this week.

_____

_____

_____

_____

_____

Words to Memorize

For Discussion:

Your favorite memory verses:
Mom:

_____

_____

_____

Daughter:

_____
_____
_____

Your Goals for This Week

Mom:

_____
_____
_____
_____
_____
_____

Daughter:

_____
_____
_____
_____
_____

Write a Closing Prayer

_____
_____

_____

_____

_____

_____

_____

_____

_____

_____

_____

_____

Benediction

But grow in the grace and knowledge of our Lord and Savior
Jesus Christ. To him be glory both now and forever! Amen.
2 Peter 3:18

Mother:

Plan a ceremony for your daughter at home, perhaps when no one else will be home. Set up a special place for your ceremony. Decorate the area with fresh flowers, candles, or some other items. List several ways that you've seen your daughter grow during your time together in *Growing Little Women for Younger Girls.*

Photocopy an enlarged version of the "Certificate of Completion" onto special paper at a local copy shop. Make one copy for yourself and one for your daughter. Purchase identical frames for the certificates.

During your ceremony, serve your daughter's favorite dessert and discuss ways that you and she have grown through this journey. After dessert, pray together and thank God for all that He has done in your lives and in your relationship with each other and with Him.

Then present the "Certificate of Completion" to your daughter. Take turns signing each certificate, and then place them in the frames.

Certificate of Completion

*T*his is to certify that _____ and
_____ have together completed
the course of study in *Growing Little Women for
Younger Girls* on this _____ day of _____,
_____.

Signatures _____

_____

Certificate of Commitment

$\mathcal{T}$his is to certify that _____

and _____ have on this _____

day of _____, _____,

agreed to _____

_____.

       Signatures _____

                   _____

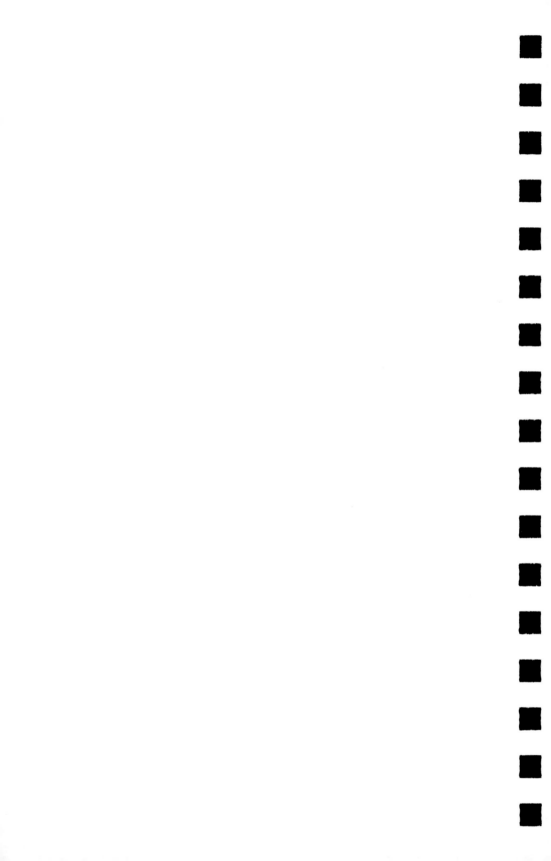

TWENTY-ONE QUESTIONS

*H*ere are 21 fun and thought-provoking questions for Mom and daughter. Use these to discover more about each other. Have fun!

1. What makes a great day for you?

   Mom:

   _____

   _____

   Daughter:

   _____

   _____

2. If you could choose one food and have as much of it as you want, but nothing else during the week, what would you choose, and why?

   Mom:

   _____

   _____

Daughter:

_____

_____

3. Which is your very favorite room in our house? Why is it your favorite?
Mom:

_____

_____

Daughter:

_____

_____

4. What is your favorite book? Why is it your favorite?
Mom:

_____

_____

_____

_____

Daughter:

_____

_____

_____

_____

5. What would you rather do . . . skate or ride a bike?
   Mom:

   _____

   Daughter:

   _____

6. Mom, who was your favorite teacher while you were in elementary school? Why was this person your favorite teacher?

   _____

   _____

   Daughter, what do you really like about your teacher this year?

   _____

   _____

7. If you could be any character from a movie, book, or any time in history, who would you be? Why?
   Mom:

   _____

   _____

   _____

   Daughter:

   _____

   _____

   _____

8. What is your favorite ice cream flavor?
Mom:

_____

Daughter:

_____

9. If you could do absolutely anything you want this Saturday, what would you do?
Mom:

_____

Daughter:

_____

10. What sport do you enjoy the most?
Mom:

_____

Daughter:

_____

11. Daughter, what is your favorite subject in school? Why?

_____
_____

Ask your mother what her favorite subject was when she
was your age.

_____
_____

12. What foreign country have you heard the most about? What do you think it would be like to grow up in that country?
    Mom:

    _____

    _____

    Daughter:

    _____

    _____

13. What is your favorite candy?
    Mom:

    _____

    Daughter:

    _____

14. Mom, what was the best birthday or Christmas present you received as a young girl?

    _____

    _____

    Daughter, what is the best present you have ever received from your mother?

    _____

    _____

15. What chore do you like the least?
Mom:

_____

_____

Daughter:

_____

_____

16. Daughter, what would you like to be when you grow up?

_____

_____

Mother, what did you think you wanted to be when you grew up?

_____

_____

17. What is your favorite board game?
Mom:

_____

Daughter:

_____

18. Would you like to have an identical twin? Why or why not? What would be the best thing about having an identical twin? What would be the worst thing?

Mom:

_____

_____

_____

Daughter:

_____

_____

_____

19. What is your favorite animal?

Mom:

_____

Daughter:

_____

20. What is your favorite family occasion? What's your favorite meal on that occasion?

Mom:

_____

_____

Daughter:

_____

_____

21. If you could do something special for one of your friends, who would it be, and what would you do?

Mom:

_____

_____

Daughter:

_____

_____

MORE FUN STUFF

Mother, you can use these ideas to add more fun to your special time together.

1. Paint T-shirts together.

2. Make cards, using construction paper, various cutout stamps, and stamp pads. Send these to relatives, friends, and shut-ins from your church or neighborhood.

3. Have a tea party for just the two of you—and maybe invite some of your daughter's favorite dolls.

4. Buy a package of thick, colored chalk and have fun creating sidewalk art. If your daughter doesn't know how to play hopscotch, teach her. If she knows how and you don't remember, have her teach you.

5. If your city has an arboretum, take a trip there and talk about the different flowers, plants, and trees. Enjoy God's wonderful creation.

6. Go out for ice cream.

7. Take your lunch or dinner to the park. Don't forget to play on the jungle gym.

8. Together, host a banana-split night for your family. Send each person a personal invitation.

9. Have a bubblegum-blowing contest with just the two of you.

10. Invite your daughter's schoolteacher or Sunday school teacher over for dessert. Allow your daughter to choose her favorite recipe, and make it together.

11. Have your daughter "interview" a grandmother, an aunt, or an older woman in your church. Have your daughter create her own questions. This can be a fun and educational time.

12. Do a service project together, such as raking leaves, washing a car, or walking your neighbor's dog. This would be a wonderful way to encourage an older person in your church or neighborhood.

13. Spend time looking at photo albums from your daughter's life and your life.

14. If your daughter has a new friend at school or church, have a "welcoming party" for her.

15. Plant a vegetable or flower garden together. Plant a bush or a tree together that will grow quickly over the next few years.

16. Host a party with a missions theme for the girls in your daughter's Sunday school class. Choose one particular missionary's family and find out different facts about their location and food. Maybe you can even serve this food to the girls. Include in your invitation to the party a list of small items each girl could bring that can be sent to the missionary's family. What an encouragement that would be to the missionaries as you capture a teachable moment with your daughter and her friends.

17. Create your own bookmarks for your friends and family. Use different-colored felt or construction paper.

18. Have a Talent Show night. Each of you take turns show-casing the things you do well and talk about why you each enjoy these things.

19. Interview each other on videotape. This will be a trea-sured memory.

20. Have a game night where your daughter gets to choose the games that you'll play for a full hour.

21. Pick up fast food for your daughter and surprise her at school for lunch. Or "kidnap" your daughter and take her to lunch on a schoolday.

SINCE 1894, Moody Publishers has been dedicated to equip and motivate people to advance the cause of Christ by publishing evangelical Christian literature and other media for all ages, around the world. Because we are a ministry of the Moody Bible Institute of Chicago, a portion of the proceeds from the sale of this book go to train the next generation of Christian leaders.

If we may serve you in any way in your spiritual journey toward understanding Christ and the Christian life, please contact us at www.moodypublishers.com.

"All Scripture is God-breathed and is useful for teaching, rebuking, correcting and training in righteousness, so that the man of God may be thoroughly equipped for every good work."

—*2 Timothy 3:16, 17*

MOODY
PUBLISHERS

THE NAME YOU CAN TRUST®

We'd love to hear from you!

If you have any questions or suggestions
feel free to contact us at:

Donna J Miller
506 Gretchen Ct
Greensboro NC 27410

Mentoring for Moms

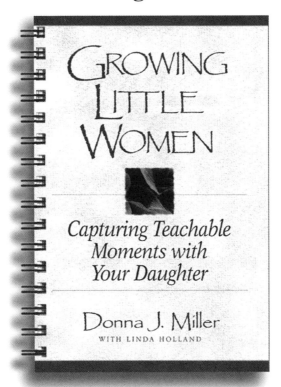

Growing Little Women
Capturing Teachable Moments with Your Daughter

To combat constant media and peer pressure, Donna Miller offers
mothers and their special young ladies easy-to-understand, teachable moments from God's Word. Designed to catch those fleeting
moments before a girl becomes a woman, this workbook will
bond mother and daughter in the love of God.

Designed for girls ages 9 to 12.

Spiral 0-8024-2185-7

MOODY
The Name You Can Trust
1-800-678-8812 www.MoodyPress.org